ADVANCE PRAISE

"*Side Hustle to Main Hustle* combines meaningful storytelling, real world experiences, and practical advice to give women a road map to go from straddling the fence to full-time entrepreneurship. If you are a woman who is ready to make the leap, this is the book to read!"

— Angela C. Dingle
CEO, Ex Nihilo

"No matter if you're a seasoned business owner or a start-up entrepreneur who feels lost and alone, this book finds you and brings you home... back to the grind and hustle."

— Gloria Blackmon
Aspiring entrepreneur

"*Side Hustle to Main Hustle* is hands down the best guidebook for entrepreneurs with a sprinkle of magical insight that has me excited about discovering my innate gifts and implementing the BEAST mentality methodology."

— Ashley Queen-Monterio
CEO, 3 Vines Consulting

T0062010

"*Side Hustle to Main Hustle* is the perfect compass for persons en route from (un)employment to owning a successful business. Get ready to be immersed in every word, story, and lesson as you journey through the pages of entrepreneurship with Angel Livas."

— Bradisha Fraser
CEO, Cay Focus Photography

Side Hustle to Main Hustle

SIDE
HUSTLE
to
MAIN
HUSTLE

The Owner's Manual to
FULL-TIME ENTREPRENEURSHIP

ANGEL N. LIVAS

NEW YORK

LONDON • NASHVILLE • MELBOURNE • VANCOUVER

Side Hustle to Main Hustle

The Owner's Manual to Full-Time Entrepreneurship

Published in New York, New York, by Morgan James Publishing in partnership with Difference Press. Morgan James is a trademark of Morgan James, LLC. www.MorganJamesPublishing.com

ISBN 9781631951077 paperback
ISBN 9781631951084 eBook
ISBN 9781631951091 audio
Library of Congress Control Number: 2020934595

Cover Design and Interior Design: Chris Treccani www.3dogcreative.net

Editor: Cory Hott

Book Coaching: The Author Incubator

Morgan James is a proud partner of Habitat for Humanity Peninsula and Greater Williamsburg. Partners in building since 2006.

Get involved today! Visit
MorganJamesPublishing.com/giving-back

I'm forever grateful to my village for believing in my vision and making me a better person throughout the process. This one's for my King and my Knight.

TABLE OF CONTENTS

FOREWORD

reat ideas come a dime a dozen. It's effective planning, execution, and the willingness to fail that sets successful people apart from mere idea generators. For as long as I can remember I've told people that success is pretty much determined by the obstacles you overcome in life, not by the positions or the titles that you hold. It's refreshing to see that a millennial has grasped this concept and is willing to share it with her counterparts and the rest of the world.

When I first met Angel, she had recently launched her business, DC Media Connection, based in Washington, DC. She was on business travel in Atlanta, Georgia, where she was attending the HOPE Global Forums to connect with global business leaders. From a glance, you could tell that she was serious about her business. However, it was her ability to understand the needs of others that was the most appealing quality that I grasped, immediately.

As a business owner, it's imperative that you understand that your work isn't about you; it's about the lives that you impact. It's your job to determine how your product or service makes the lives of others better.

At a young age, I learned that in order for me to win the support of my community, I had to show up for my community. This proved to be true throughout my time as the associate director of the Georgia Democratic Party and even more so when I was named the first African-American State Director under U.S. Senator Sam Nunn. When I accepted the position as National Chairman of 100 Black Men of America, it was yet another step towards creating impact while connecting to the most important capital you can have…people.

In business you will rely on people to push your initiative or movement forward. Whether it's through your interior support team (i.e., your mentors, coaches, et cetera) or your forward-facing team (i.e., staff, volunteers, et cetera) you will need to understand what your vision is, before you can expect anyone else to assist you. Throughout *Side Hustle to Main Hustle*, you will be introduced to a step-by-step blueprint to building a sustainable business. Whether you have been managing your side business for two years or twelve. You will gain the necessary footing you need to transition into full-time entrepreneurship.

The B.E.A.S.T Mentality methodology constructed by Angel is a necessity to building your internal confidence, preparing your business structure, developing your annual projections, selecting your support team, and operating from a space of authenticity.

One of the hardest realities I had to face before launching the TWD Conglomerate was learning that I would never be paid my worth, while working for someone else. No matter how much a company sings your praises or tells you they love you, you will never be compensated for your true value. That's why my road to success has been centered around planning, making my own investments, minding my own businesses, all while recognizing that I am ultimately responsible for the success of my business ventures and making my dreams reality.

As the chief executive officer of six different businesses—TWD, Inc., a private sector consulting firm; FAD Consulting, LLC, a public sector consulting firm that works closely with Hartsfield-Jackson Atlanta International Airport, U.S. Department of Transportation, and the U.S. Department of Energy; Atlanta Transportation Systems Inc., a non-emergency para-transit system; Better Dreams Mattress Manufacturing Company; Southwest Investment Group; and LANCOR Parking Inc.—I understand the importance of creating business processes, structures and projection planning.

Congratulations on taking the first step towards gaining the core elements to transition successfully into full-time business ownership. While this is a great launching pad, it is up to you to do the work. The moment that you realize that success is a journey, and not a destination, you will naturally begin to maneuver differently.

Over the past five years, I have watched Angel create a space for others to build, grow, and excel throughout their entrepreneurial journey. Hundreds of men and women have attended her business events across the world and most people agree that they leave more knowledgeable and connected than when they first arrived. I believe that if you are ready to transition yourself into a full-time business owner you have selected the perfect book. If this book teaches you nothing else, it should impart wisdom about the importance of investing in yourself and the willingness to bet 100 percent on you, even when everyone else has counted you out.

Thomas W. Dortch, Jr., CEO, TWD, Inc.
Author of *The Miracles of Mentoring:*
The Joy of Investing in Our Future
Atlanta, GA

CHAPTER 1:

Straddling the Fence

"What would you do if you weren't afraid?"
– SHERYL SANDBERG

There are people who are placed in our lives for a purpose and others we merely choose to allow on our journey. I believe that my line sister, from the illustrious Alpha Kappa Alpha Sorority, Incorporated, was orchestrated to be in my life. She grew up as an only child in Saudi Arabia; however, today she calls Virginia home. It's the place that she and her husband, a member of Kappa Alpha Psi Fraternity, decided to raise their two amazing kids. She works hard and continues to strive for excellence as she climbs the corporate ladder. At the end of the day, her job pays the bills and allows her to live a successful life. Not just in the traditional sense, either. She's a stellar mom, supportive wife, compassionate daughter, and an amazing friend. Yet somehow she still manages to feel as if something is missing.

My halfsie, as I affectionately call my line sister, is the epitome of a responsible adult. She considers her options carefully and only makes moves after thoroughly calculating her risks. Before marriage and the kids, she dreamed of traveling the world and working in some form of foreign services. For instance, she would have been an amazing diplomat or even United States Ambassador. But then the reality of what it would take to live out her dreams set in…and well, things change. She had to make some hard decisions. Either opt for a life that would make it nearly impossible to settle down and have a family or put her dreams on hold to fulfill the life that she could live with, while also making her family and friends proud.

Ultimately, she chose the latter and was content with her decision; however, a small part of her wanted more. She researched a few possible business ideas but, got stuck in the "learning" phase. She participated in seminars, dozens of online webinars, purchased memberships, and yet she couldn't seem to get past the "gathering information" phase. She read books, scheduled meetings with potential clients to understand their needs, yet something held her back from officially launching her business.

Now, some might say that it would be absolutely ludicrous to leave your corporate career (i.e., steady paycheck) for an idea and a hunch that your business venture will work. But, at some point you have to trust yourself enough to own the path that God has laid before you…no matter how crazy it might seem. This isn't to say that you don't need vision and a strategy, because you do. But, you also have to be willing to do the hard work of putting your research and knowledge into tangible actions.

One day, while I was talking with my line sister about her craft room, a sacred space that she builds and manages her crafting projects, I realized that her passion for arts and crafts could actually be a lucrative side business. It wouldn't require her to research anything because she loves creating homemade cards, scrapbooks and other artsy projects. It was the perfect side hustle to ease her into becoming familiar and comfortable with entrepreneurship.

That's where she started. Plus, unbeknown to me, she already had certifications as a crafter—who knew there was such a thing. Her side hustle met her in a space that she was comfortable and already well-versed in the products, pricing, and potential clients. So, she started small, selling a variety of special occasion cards to friends and family. Eventually she started hosting classes to teach adults how to make scrapbooks, holiday cards, and other specialty craft projects. As her confidence grew, so did her visibility. She launched her social media pages to highlight her artistic projects and she was super excited about posting (for all of two months), and then she found herself right where she started. Unenthused. Tired. Wanting more, and back to researching the business idea she's been sleeping on for years.

My line sister couldn't just up and walk away from corporate America, because she's responsible. No sane, responsible person would leave their "good job" to pursue entrepreneurship. Who in their right mind would leave the financial security of a guaranteed paycheck for the uncertainty of not knowing how much money you may or may not make?

Then there are the voices of your family and friends who will surely question your sanity if you decided to walk away from it all. Trust me, I know. Their doubts fuel you to stay within a safe space, because you can't handle the ridicule if you gave up on everything and it doesn't work. How will you ever face your family or friends? They will laugh. They will talk, and you just might lose a few of them along the way.

You start a side hustle. In this case, my line sister allowed her passion to direct the path of her business. She started selling products, teaching classes, and doing an amazing job growing her side hustle.

It is possible to become content with managing a side business alongside your full-time job. Well, that's what you tell yourself to calm down all the negative chatter that seems to take over your psyche.

As I said earlier, I believe God ordains certain people to come into your life. Just like my line sister was called to be in my life to teach me many lessons, I believe I was guided to walk in her path. I've been able to help show her the possibilities of what can happen if you ever decide you're ready to walk in your purpose completely.

The beautiful thing about our relationship is she's watched me grow as an entrepreneur. She's been there for my wins and my setbacks. Yet, through it all, she keeps me motivated and pressing forward. I know she has what it takes to see the true manifestations of her heart come to life. You know those silent thoughts you keep self-contained that you only allow to come out to play when you feel like you are in a safe space? What if I told you it's possible to transition your side hustle to your main hustle and, better yet, into your full-time business?

I know it's possible because I've helped several people in this position soar as entrepreneurs. A year or so ago, one of my clients, Bianca Wise, was the first African-American lieutenant for the Baltimore Fire Department. She had the type of entrepreneurial mind that made her ready to leap, but she just wanted some guidance to help her along the way. I was so proud of her because despite the position, the title, and the money, she had gotten to a place where she was ready to bet one hundred percent on herself.

Today, my client has two phenomenal businesses. One is hobby-based, and the other is based on passion. Bianca utilized the tools from our sessions to make the transition. I wanted to share Bianca's story because, like many women, on the outside, it looked like she had everything, but not on the inside. If your soul is crying out to do more or be more, you must answer the calling. You won't feel satisfied until you do.

It's not uncommon for entrepreneurs to have multiple businesses. My mentor once asked me if I wanted my business to be a lifestyle business or a money-generating business. Of course, I chose the latter, but "feel good" businesses can also be lucrative.

About three years ago, I decided I wanted to create a platform for women business owners to have a safe space to learn, grow, and share their entrepreneurial experience. Going into it, I had no desire to start another business. But shortly after our first event, which had nearly 150 women registered to attend, I realized there was a need for what I was doing. That is how my second business, The Woman Behind The Business®, which is a 501c(3), was born. There are a number of ways for you to build your business. There is no right way—the only directive is you must start.

Imagine being like my friend. Leisel, a real estate beast. She joined me on my radio show, The Woman Behind the Business talk show, which airs on 96.3FM-HD4 in Washington, DC, and is now available on podcast! At one point, she shared how she could barely afford to pay for her son's formula back when we used to work together at AARP. She and her husband were working, but they just couldn't find a way to make ends meet. She would crawl into work at wee hours of the morning to study for her realtor's license. Once she got her license, she was using those early mornings to create marketing materials for her business. She realized it would be too hard for her to straddle the careers too long, so she chose to soar. She chose to bet one hundred percent on herself and today she is one of the top producers at Keller Williams Realty.

What is the potential for your story? How do you want your story to play out? I want to be able to include your transitional story in one of my upcoming trainings or seminars. You don't have to keep straddling the fence. You can make a commitment to choose you and the vision that's been placed on your heart. I am a firm believer that God gives each of us visions, but it's up to us to work to build them out. I know if he gives us the vision; he won't stop there. He'll also provide the provisions for us to be successful. But, you can't just sit around waiting for something magical to happen, you have to put in work.

Have you ever decided to do something for someone who couldn't decide if they wanted to go in one direction over another? Well, you know if they work with you, you will be one hundred percent committed to their success. Whatever resources you need to put in their path or investments you need to make, you are committed to doing so, but because the person is teetering and hasn't fully committed, you stop taking them seriously. You start to shift your attention to people who are more respectful of your time.

I think this is similar to how you attract what you want from the Universe. If you're serious and ready to trust the process, the Universe will be there to provide you with everything you need to be successful, but you have to be ready. You have to be intentional with your requests and purposeful with your walk. When you act according to the desires of your heart, you can and will manifest abundance in ways beyond your wildest dreams.

The quote that led you into this chapter could not have been more perfect. Sheryl Sandberg once said, "What would you do if you weren't afraid?" I think it's such a simple, yet profound question. Many people walk around operating from a place of fear, and it's so debilitating. You have so much potential, but you allow your mind to control your progress, and ultimately it stifles you. You allow the fear of what others might say control your output, instead of considering the cons of not reaching your greatest potential.

Don't get me wrong, I know you have fears. We all do. The difference is you probably attempt to justify most of them and defend the others as if your life depends on it. The Bible says, that "God didn't give us a spirit of fear" (2 Timothy 1:7 WEB). Do you believe that faith and fear can't coexist? If so, which is stronger for you? And if it's fear—have you identified what your fears are? Is it money? If so, I get it. But, can I tell you a little secret? You will make it. Here's how I know.

I was married for nine years. He was with me through my high times, and we divorced when I was probably at my lowest. I have been in business for four and a half years, and overall business is great, but going through a divorce in the midst of having a fairly new business wasn't an easy feat. Everything that had been my constant turned into uncharted waters. Money seemed to come and go as quickly as I was making it. Still, I managed to rent a new house, pay my kid's private school tuition, and do as much "normal" as I knew possible.

If money is holding you back from living your best life, then you must not want it bad enough. Building a business takes sacrifice, the ability to plan, money management, and the willingness to humble yourself. If you're building a business for an opportunity to show off or just to let the world know how great you are, you're doing it with the wrong intentions. You should want to scale your business because you know there are people out there in need of what you're selling or offering.

Society doesn't need another arrogant business owner who just wants to show off how amazing they are. Our world is in need of leaders or business owners with a servant's heart. Society needs individuals who want to do good in the world and want the universe to benefit from their innate gifts.

What are your innate gifts, you ask? Well, they are the things you seem to be able to do without guidance, direction, or instruction. They are part of your natural abilities. For instance, when I was a child, I used to organize plays for my family to attend on Sunday evenings, and I put on a show. Somehow, I talked my two siblings into being the stars of the show, while I directed and handled all of the marketing. It was great. I created tickets, complete with the barcode scanner. The attendees received program books organized by scene, and it came complete with a personal invitation. This is something I had been doing since I was about eight years old. Fast-forward almost thirty years, and that's in such alignment with my career. No one ever taught me how to do those things; they came naturally to me. They are part of my innate gifts.

Do you know what your innate gifts are? Try to recall some of your early memories. Can you think of some things you enjoyed doing that were second nature to you? Now, I want you to think about your side-hustle. Does it have anything to do with your innate gifts? If you're interested in starting a business, does your business idea align with one of your natural gifts? If not, it doesn't mean you shouldn't go into business. However, I do believe if your passion is in alignment with your innate gifts, well then, you're walking in your purpose. Which, in turn, means you're in alignment with your earthly calling.

Let's go back to my line sister for a second. She has all of the aesthetics of living a bountiful life. I know, in time, she will make it to exactly where she wants to be as a business owner. I believe that researching your industry is incredibly important, as it helps you learn ahead of the curve instead of while you're going through it. I'm so happy to know that, when the time is right, she'll be well versed in her industry to build and maintain success. I'm also ecstatic to know that she is not rushing into something. And I'll know, whenever it happens, that I played an integral role in her transition from employee to full-time boss.

I know she is one of my greatest fans. I also know that the same greatness, happiness, and fulfillment she seeks for me in my life, I desire for her. Now, I don't doubt that she is successful and happy. But when you're walking in your purpose, it's a different kind of happiness. Your appreciation for time becomes magnified. Your value becomes undeniable. Your purpose? Well, you own that.

Your life dials up from contentment to fulfillment. The same light you once saw in people you admired well, you're now radiating it at your highest frequency. The best part about it is that you know you are. You're operating from a place of great intention, and now, when people come in contact with you, they're attracted to your energy. Your passion begins to shine through in everything you do. People want to hear what you have to say because they can see the passion behind every word. You'll be able to walk into rooms you never knew you'd ever enter because you're taking ownership of the magnificent person that you are.

You're no longer worried about what people are saying about you because they have now joined the bandwagon. They will tell you they always knew you had it in you (but, only after you make it). We'll dive into your support system a little later in Chapter 7. But for now, just know that they mean well.

Regardless, all of these reasons that you're still on the fence—it just means that you still have trepidation about relinquishing the B.E.A.S.T. It's inside of you, trust me. By the end of this book, you'll know just what you need to do to release it.

CHAPTER 2:

Leaning Not on My Own Understanding

"I've got a dream that's worth more than my sleep."
– Unknown

had to be about thirteen years old. I was a freshman in high school, and my father managed one of the Detroit Free Press warehouses. One day, he mentioned to me and my brother that a number of employees needed help stuffing their papers, which entailed adding the weekly sales ads to the main paper. According to my dad, the workers would pay me about three cents per paper, which didn't sound like a lot, but I was open. Initially, I didn't calculate costs because it wasn't about the money for me. I just enjoyed being with my dad.

However, the first time I tried it, I made over $300 in one day. I was beyond thrilled. From that day forward, I was determined to go to work with my dad. I had built up a regular clientele and honestly, besides babysitting neighborhood kids, that was my first taste of entrepreneurship. It's funny to look back on your experiences to understand where you developed your willpower and determination. For instance, my dad always told my siblings and me to always have a side hustle. His version went a little something like this:

> *"You shouldn't put all your efforts into a company that you don't own.*
>
> *You'll make them lots of money. And at any given time, they can come to you and say, 'Thank you for sharing your talents with us, but we no longer need your services.'"*

The funny thing is, my dad was absolutely right. Unfortunately, one day I was on the receiving end of one of those conversations. It was 2014. My son, Nelson, had just turned two months old. I was sitting in my living room, and the baby had just gone down for a nap. I was finally enjoying a little peace and quiet. Then, the phone rang. It was my office calling, so I answered to make sure everything was okay. At the time, I was the executive producer for six nationally syndicated talk shows. Essentially, I always made myself available to ensure the programming was running smoothly, even during a time I was technically on leave. Well, to my surprise, this call had nothing to do with the shows. The gentleman on the other end of the phone was calling to inform me that my last day with the company would be December 8, 2014.

I was shocked. I didn't understand what was happening, especially since he started the conversation off by saying, "Angel, you know you are a total rock star." (Me: side eye, like don't butter me up to merely slam me down.) I got off the phone feeling deflated for all of about sixty seconds. Not that I was counting, but it wasn't long at all. Then, I had this euphoric moment. My mind took me back to when I first got hired. I was having a conversation with my boss in the hallway when he told me, "Don't get stuck here. You're going to make great money, and you're going to do some marvelous things, but the rest of the world needs your talents." When my subconscious recalled that memory, I felt a sense of peace come over me.

Then, I heard a voice say, "Angel, I had to do this in order for you to be who I created you to be." It was at that moment that all of my concerns, worries, and fears went out the window. I no longer looked at the situation as if I had lost my job. I looked at it as if my wings had been clipped so I could soar to new heights. I didn't know what I was going to do, since I was the breadwinner of my household, and we now had two little boys under the age of two. But, I trusted the process.

After searching for a job for a few months, I finally settled on the idea that working for someone else for less money than I was accustomed to making just wasn't an option. I wanted to do something that I loved, and I wanted to help people. I can remember having a serious "come to Jesus" moment with myself. I essentially said, "Why can't I do all the things I was doing for this huge company for my company?" And sure enough, imposter syndrome showed up to add to the conversation—reminding me that I didn't have a big brand like my previous company, so who would listen to me? It was then that I remembered all of the contacts, accolades, and relationships I'd made over my fifteen years in the industry. So, I started reminding myself of some of my greatest achievements—like being the executive producer for such Emmy award-winning hosts as Larry King and Jane Pauley. I had to really settle my nerves, and I essentially did it by reminding myself that the opportunities might have come by way of the company, but the interactions and quality of work—well, those things were all unique to me.

I guess you can say that I had to put imposter syndrome in its place, and soon after, DC Media Connection was born. It was one of the most rewarding moments of my life. I know fear is often an emotion that people feel when they branch out into entrepreneurship full-time, but I was never scared, per se. Maybe because my husband, at the time, was working, so I had some source of comfort in addition to a severance package, which essentially gave me a decent salary for about six to eight months. After that, I knew I had to be prepared to sink or swim.

Within my first three months, I won my first contract for nearly $100,000. I was stoked. This was huge for me.

I had brought on two subcontracting companies to ensure the contract ran smoothly. However, I was so excited about the project that I made some terrible mistakes from the beginning. First, the lady who owned the company was my direct contact, and she would contact me at all hours of the day and night, it did not matter. The problem was I was so eager to gain her trust and to ensure that she was happy that I accepted the calls, made last-minute modifications per her requests, and was at her beck and call for the duration of the contract. I learned a valuable lesson throughout that year: set boundaries.

Boundaries aren't just necessary for your clients; they're essential for you to maintain a positive work/life balance. I also learned that when you're running a business you can't just do things based on your internal schedule or process. You have to have a strategic approach to everything you do. While I am an organized person, this client wanted project management flow charts for all of the contractors. Now, project management flow charts were completely outside of my scope, so I found myself Googling what they were and how they worked.

I'm a creative, what can I say? Let me be clear. Charts, budgets, and micromanaging are just not my strong suits. However, once I understood the importance of having a project flow management tool, I quickly learned how to manage one. It's still not my favorite tool, but it provides your clients real-time tracking of their program or project. Now, let's go back to these budgets. While I despise keeping track of profits and losses, we were able to close out her project under budget, which saved her a little money. I'm sharing these things because I want you to know that the struggle is real for everyone, even me. When I first started in business, I didn't know how to do everything, but I did know my why. I knew why I wanted to be a business owner. I knew the impact I wanted my business to have and the legacy I wanted it to create for my family.

Growing up, I was fortunate to see both of my parents in an entrepreneurial light. They launched their real estate company, Todd's Real Estate Investments & Rentals, back in 1980—nearly forty years ago. There were periods of my childhood where my mom stayed home to take care of my siblings and me, but when she wasn't home, she owned various businesses. As an adult, I recognize the impact my parents' career choices had on my life, which is a huge part of my why. I want my children to see what hard work looks like and understand the benefits of it. I want them to possess a desire to have their own businesses, just as my parents desired for my brother and sister and me to. One of my clients is 100 Black Men of Greater Washington. Their motto is something along the lines of, "They can be what they can see." I think it's such a powerful slogan because it's one hundred percent accurate. I desire for my children to be exposed to much more than just me or their dad merely going to work to collect a paycheck. I want them to see what it looks like to believe in yourself wholeheartedly, because that's what entrepreneurship takes. You can't straddle entrepreneurship and a full-time job and expect to receive abundance. You have to lean into it carrying all your hopes, dreams, fears, and anxieties. Believing that your commitment and sacrifice will reap great return and your business will be blessed.

You Didn't See This Coming

Entrepreneurship isn't for everyone. If your sole interest is money, when things get hard and your back is against the wall, you're more than likely going to crack because money isn't a true substance. Meaning it's not strong enough to keep you going, especially if you aren't making any money. If you think back to my first story when I went to work with my dad, I didn't go for the money. I went because I wanted to spend time with my dad. If you're truly passionate about your business idea, side hustle, or start-up, the money will come, but it's your love for what you're offering the world that's going to keep you motivated when your bills are due, and you're not sure if your client is going to pay on time.

It's passion that's going to drive you to get out of bed at 4:00 a.m. to get an early start on a proposal. It's love that's going to keep you going when you're told no a thousand times. You see, I'm not going to sugar coat things or make entrepreneurship look like a nicely packaged "for sale" item. It takes grit, determination, passion, love, humility, time, persistence, and so much more. If you're not doing it with any of those traits in your back pocket, this isn't for you. But, if you are amped up because you know you are excited about your product, not because you made it, but because you know that it's something that will be a blessing to others, get ready to go on one of the most amazing journeys of your life. As you can see, my journey hasn't been perfect. But I've learned from my shortcomings to ensure that I can bring greater value to each new client and to every new circumstance.

Something to Think About

Have you identified your why? Are you ready to lean into your destiny? What character traits do you possess to help you throughout your entrepreneurial journey? How do you handle adversities?

CHAPTER 3:

Relinquish the B.E.A.S.T.

"Entrepreneurship is living a few years of your life like most people won't, so that you can spend the rest of your life like most people can't."
— Unknown

I f you breezed by the opening quote of this chapter, it's imperative that you stop right here and go back to the top of the page to re-read it. I don't know who the author of the quote is, but it's one of the most realistic quotes I've encountered about entrepreneurship. At the core of what I find the author saying is that successful people are willing to make the necessary sacrifices. And to be honest, that's the variable that's missing between those who live in mediocrity and those who decide to release the reigns to soar to their greatest potential.

I'm curious, what does success look like to you? Have you ever thought about it? Is it a dollar amount, or is it a certain way of life you want to create? I want you to take five minutes to identify three ideal success scenarios for you and your business. Once you're done, I'd like for you to meditate on those scenarios for the next three minutes (one minute each). Visualize what obstacles and blessings each scenario would bring.

Pause.

Did you enjoy seeing yourself happy, free, and living a prosperous life. Now, I want you to consider how much you're willing to sacrifice to ensure that you're able to manifest each scenario. Hopefully, you're willing to stand in agreement with your visions, because they're all possible. If your mind was able to conceptualize it, your body can bring it to fruition.

I recently traveled to Accra, Ghana. While I was there, a friend and I traveled about two hours outside of the capital to go hiking in Bonti Falls. Our goal was to reach one of the tallest peaks to behold the magical Umbrella Rock. We had attempted to trek the unbeaten path the previous year, but the weather prohibited us from completing the hike. This time, however, we made it to the top. Completely fatigued and out of breath from climbing the mountain (I was probably way out of shape), a sense of rejuvenation replenished me when I inhaled the scenic views.

A handful of local children greeted us once we reached the top. It was apparent that they didn't have much. They were without shoes and their houses looked as if they were merely built to protect them from the great outdoors. The roofs were made of a thin aluminum, and the walls were made of red clay. The children looked happy and were friendly and polite and honestly, appeared to have everything they needed. A few hours later, we returned to the capital city and stopped at a local restaurant before heading back to our hotel. While I was waiting for my food, I noticed a beautiful, well-dressed toddler who was climbing and playing on her parents. Just like the children in the village, she was happy, vibrant, and living without a care in the world. A typical toddler, right? Well, I'm not sure what happened to me, but for a brief second I had to pause and digest what I was feeling. At that moment, I wondered about the sacrifices of the ancestors or grandparents or even the parents of the little girl who was sitting in the restaurant with me.

Then, I thought about the sacrifices that my ancestors and parents made to afford me the opportunities that I've had and will continue to have. And out of nowhere, I cried. Now if you know me at all, you know how abnormal that moment must have been for me because one, I'm not a sensitive person, and two, I had a hard time comprehending the drastic shift in lifestyles that occurred after a two-hour drive.

You know society often says that people have equal opportunities, regardless of their socio-economic status. However, the reality is that everyone doesn't have equivalent starting points. The playing field isn't equal for your children or for you.

There at that moment, I thought about my two sons. I thought about the sacrifices I'm willing to make for them and whether it's enough. I often find myself pushing myself to the limit because I know there is someone else out there who has closed their eyes and envisioned a better tomorrow for themselves and their family, and yes, they're willing to make the sacrifice. People can't be mad if someone else works harder to accomplish their dreams. Everyone has different starting points, but the one thing that everyone has in common is determining how hard you're willing to push, how long you're going to work, and how much you're willing to sacrifice.

That person you visualized enjoying the benefits of your hard work already exists. They're already there. That's how I know it's possible. You just tapped into your future self and asked to see what is possible with a little hard work and a few sacrifices.

It's amazing how in tune children are when you take the time to explain things and teach them. My children have been asking to go on a Disney Cruise for over a year. I wanted to wait until they were both at an age that they would remember the experience. Now that my youngest is five and my oldest is six, I figured this would be a good year for them to go. Now, I decided this before I started going through a divorce, but I wasn't going to allow that situation to cause us to have to postpone the trip. So, I'm completely transparent with the boys. Whenever they ask about the trip, I explain that Mommy is working hard to generate additional income so we can still go on the trip.

I also suggest that we set them up a business—but they have to identify a few different business ideas for us to select from.

Anyway, fast forward to mid-September, just after my son, Nelson's, last birthday. My sister gave him a card and some money. When he saw the money, he got excited. I walked with him to his room to ensure he placed it in his piggy bank. But, before we could get to the room he took the money and said, "Here, Mommy, this is for you. You can use it to help pay for the Disney Cruise." I was so humbled by his thoughtful nature that I cried (I promise you I'm not a cry baby, y'all. I'm not). I told him I had already paid for the trip and that he could use his money to pay for something he wants while we're on the trip. He didn't argue with that. So, I put his money in his piggy bank and walked out of his room so full of pride.

I was so proud of him for making the gesture. It just goes to show that kids listen and understand a lot more than they are given credit for. I don't think my kids are an exception to any rules. However, I do applaud myself for taking the time to teach my children about entrepreneurship, about saving money, and about the power of togetherness. The same skills that I've crafted in the B.E.A.S.T. Mentality are the skills that I share with my boys about business. I want to change the trajectory of how individuals look at business and doing business. There is no time better than the present to start implementing new ideas. There is no time like right now for you to begin making a positive transformation in your life. You just have to decide you're worth the commitment. If you're ready, I'm ready, too. I'll meet you right where you are to guide you directly to the place you want to be.

When I first developed the B.E.A.S.T. Mentality phrase, I wanted to understand the difference between how men and women handled business. My mentor, Angela C. Dingle, CEO of Ex Nihilo, once told the story about how differently she and her ex-husband would network, even at family events. Let's say that they were off at a child's birthday party she noticed that the women would be off discussing the children and other life events, while the men would be discussing business. Likewise, at business networking events, she observed that men would talk about business while the women would compliment each other on clothing or accessories. She explained that research has shown that men and women network differently. Men often walk away from a networking event with a recommendation for an attorney, broker, or banker, but a woman might walk away with a recommendation for a great stylist or a pair of shoes. And so the way a woman engages with her peers is important.

The first time I heard it, I started tracking how I engaged with other women—and men, for that matter. I noticed I was a victim of her case study. I would notice a woman's shoes or outfit, and more than likely, I'd compliment her on it. But, here's how I was slightly different: I used that compliment as an introduction to engage with the individual. I utilized the compliment as part of my highlight (or this is how you should remember me) when I follow-up with individuals. However, I recognized that everyone did not use the same tactic. Most people would let the conversation stop there. Which is why I incorporate effective networking into the B.E.A.S.T. Mentality methodology. I shifted the focus from how men and women conduct business to strategically assist them in transitioning from the workplace to entrepreneurship. Allow me to introduce you to elements that make up having a B.E.A.S.T. Mentality.

Believe

Greatness stems from believing that you are enough. But what does that look like? I know a lot of people say they believe in themselves. Do they know what that means? We'll examine your why and dive into the root of your beliefs and help you transition any self-doubts to victories.

Execute

Do you have what it takes to plan like a boss? Not just use the sexy language, but be efficient with your planning efforts. There are a lot of i's to be dotted and t's to be crossed when you're structuring a business properly. Throughout this phase, you will evaluate each of those elements to ensure you are structurally sound and that you're building a business that's sustainable and can make a difference.

Account

No, you won't just learn about money in this phase. However, it is all about accountability. When you officially build a business, it's not just about you. You're now responsible for your workers being able to feed their families, so accountability matters. This phase is broken into two sub-categories: Do Your Dollars Make Sense and Marketing Strategies That Work. You'll want to spend a lot of time understanding this phase, while also converting the tactics into practical tools for your business.

Support

Building your village is one of the key ingredients to maintaining your entrepreneurial stamina. These are the people who keep you going on days that you just want to throw in the towel. Trust me, you'll have days like that. Whether it's a mentor, your team members, or your roster of cheerleaders, everyone needs a strong support base. We recently touched on the importance of networking effectively; however, the surface hasn't even been scratched. By the end of this chapter, you'll have a better understanding of why it's important to surround yourself with the right people to move your vision forward.

Transparent

Transparency is what separates an amazing businessperson from the pack. It's necessary to own your truth. When it comes to your business, the brand is only as good as its leadership team. To me, a brand is an extension of its founder. If you are transparent about the dealings of the company, it will evoke trust and, in turn, a positive relationship with its customers. This is where you have the ability to take the market by storm and win people over with your authentic character and business acumen.

There you have it, The B.E.A.S.T. Mentality is made up of five key elements:

1. Believe: You Are Enough
2. Execute: Plan Like A Boss
3. Account: Mind Your Business
4. Support: Build Your Village
5. Transparent: Walk In Your Truth

Throughout each of these phases, it's important that you take the time to process how you can see yourself implementing the information outlined in the forthcoming chapters. Grab a pen and a notepad that you'll name "B.E.A.S.T. Mentality," and get ready for us to go on a journey to transition your side-hustle into your full-time business. If this is truly the direction your soul is tugging you toward, congratulations for taking the first step and reading up to this point. Now, in order for this transition to work, we must be in sync. You have to be willing to receive the information I have for you. If you're ready, I'm so excited to embark upon this journey with you. Us connecting here was no accident. Embrace the possibilities of what can be. Let's dive into preparing your heart, mind, and body to become one with having a B.E.A.S.T. Mentality.

CHAPTER 4:

Believe—You Are Enough

"The man on top of the mountain didn't fall there."
— Vince Lombardi

f I asked you to craft a detailed business plan that's a minimum of fifty pages—which highlights your target audience, financial structure, marketing plan, along with your business mission, vision, and service offerings—within twenty-four hours, would you get it done? For most people, they would make an excuse and say it's too much to get done in such a short amount of time. Plus, there's no incentive for getting it done, aside from you having your business plan completed, right?

Well, now let's say I asked for the same thing, except this time I show you a check for $1.5 million (that doesn't have to be paid back) and tell you it's yours if you can meet the deadline. Would you get it done?

31

I don't know what you might have had planned for the next twenty-four hours, but I'm pretty certain that for $1.5 million, you'd figure out a work-around to ensure you met the deadline. There are a number of reasons why your second response would more than likely differ from the first request, but one of the biggest reasons is because your "why" shifted. In the first ask, you probably didn't even consider adjusting your schedule to adhere to the request because the need wasn't beneficial enough. However, in the second scenario, you were probably organizing a team in your head before an agreement was even signed. This is how powerful your why needs to be. It has to move you to want to take action with the same level of urgency as $1.5 million.

For some unforeseen reason, I believe that our why is uniquely tied to how much we believe in ourselves. Sticking with the example above, when the latter option was presented to you, at any point did you think, Oh, no. I can't possibly get this done? I doubt it. You'd trust yourself enough to figure it out.

I've stood in crowded rooms and asked the audience, "How many people here believe in themselves?" In an instant, all of the hands in the room typically will fly up in the air. Smirks replace blank stares and some people might even snicker at the question. Then I ask them, "Do you believe in yourself enough to walk away from the security of a steady paycheck to explore entrepreneurship?" A number of hands start to fall. But when I ask, "If I asked you to provide me a deadline for you to turn in your two-week notice, how much time would you need?" And at that moment, people typically start to look at me as if I was absolutely crazy. I can recall one person saying, "Why would I leave my well-paying job to pursue something when I don't even know if it will work?" What that individual was saying was that he didn't believe in himself enough to walk away from the structure of a nine-to-five. I think society has been conditioned to walk into corporate jobs, perform a list of tasks around our job description, and collect a check every couple of weeks. This cycle is how many people are programmed. They have essentially mastered their duties; however, they lack a desire to do anything additional within the company. This is where some people settle into complacent behavior, while others recognize their complacency and decide they want more.

Throughout this book, I'll share a lot of stories, situations, and methods. But before you can make it to digesting any of those things, you have to shift your mindset. You have to think about who you are and whose you are. This isn't a spiritual book, but it does require you to know and believe that you have a transformative power residing within you. You must also realize that it's up to you to tap into it and relinquish all of the magic you were born to sprinkle all over the world. When you know that God created you, and you are beautifully and wonderfully made, then that should tell you that you can accomplish anything you set your mind to. I encourage you to adopt the mentality expressed in the lyrics of the hit song by rapper, Bone Crusher: "I ain't never scared." You don't have to embrace the rest of the lyrics, but you shouldn't have a spirit of fear—even the bible tells us that.

However, over the years I've found that fear is the one thing that's capable of holding you back from reaching your full potential. People make excuses about what they can't do because of the timing. Well, I challenge you to start right where you are. I promise to meet you there. But first, you must operate from a spirit of fearlessness and resilience. If you're ready to change your mentality and garner the methods of acquiring the B.E.A.S.T. Mentality, then get ready to unlock the magic that you've been holding captive. If you agree that you're ready to exceedingly and abundantly reap the fruits of your labor, then take this vow:

I, _____, promise to boldly walk in my purpose. I reject self-doubt. I assertively rebuke fear, as fear and faith can't co-exist. I believe in the innate gifts I possess, and I'm committed to coupling them with hard work and determination to reach my full potential.

If you can own this pledge, then I welcome you to the first stage of gaining the B.E.A.S.T. Mentality.

Before you're ready to soar as an entrepreneur, you have to have a solid understanding of your why. Do you know why you've decided to launch your business? If your response has anything to do with immediate money, I'm going to ask you to dig deeper. The first time I heard about knowing my why, I was still working in corporate America.

I don't recall what sparked me to commit to reading at least eight books a year, but I did. The first book that I decided to read was Compound Effect, by Darren Hardy. If you haven't read it, I highly recommend it. In the book, Hardy gave an example of how strong your why has to be. I don't remember the scenario verbatim, but I'll give you my version, which will leave you with the same understanding of the message. If someone asked you to tightrope across the roof of two buildings, yet the one you're walking toward was on fire, would you do it for $10,000?

Now, I want you to consider this. What if the scenario was slightly modified to include your toddler child crying out to you from the burning roof, would you walk the tightrope then?

When I read that, I instantly thought, for my child, absolutely, there would be no question. Well, that's because the why is worth it. I'm no longer doing it for money. I'm doing it to save my child. Well, that's how I want you to construct your why. It needs to be for a reason that moves you to keep pressing forward even when everything else seems to be working against you. You need to have real, heart-tugging reasons why you want to build your business. If you start here and truly understand the root of why your business will make a difference, it will carry you through the difficult times. It will help you maintain your focus and help you persevere.

Foundation of Freedom

Fox. This simple three-letter word changed my life in a way I could have never imagined. While engaging in a conversation with an older gentleman at a Friends of The Smithsonian event, I noticed his spy museum tie held a secret message, which jumped out at me rather instantly. When I read the message aloud, the distinguished man grinned. "I'm impressed," he said. From there, things just began to flow. Throughout our conversation, he learned a number of things about me, but what seemed to interest him the most was my home state of Michigan.

During our follow-up conversations, we crafted a plan, which I thought was pretty genius. We joined forces to launch a project, which I named Foundation of Freedom. The project was centralized around commissioning a bronze bust to be created for former Congressman John J. Conyers, Jr., one of the founding members of the Congressional Black Caucus, and the man responsible for hiring civil rights legend Rosa Parks. The idea seemed perfect. We would utilize my partner's knowledge and love of art to locate a sculptor and commission the project, while tapping into my Michigan connection and project management skills to orchestrate the world's first bronze bust of any African-American in Congress—and have the work installed in the Smithsonian. If you know anything about art, then you know that the Smithsonian is the world's largest museum. It's made up of nineteen museums and the National Zoo. We were ambitious enough to craft a plan to attempt to have a piece of work installed in the prestigious institution, and the once crazy idea actually manifested in less than eight months.

Our first meeting took place in the spring of 2016 at 11:30 a.m. with the Congressman's staff at his office in the Rayburn Building on Capitol Hill. The team appeared impressed with our plan, but more importantly, interested, especially since my colleague was going to commission the project. I recall walking out of Congressman Conyers' office feeling a sense of excitement. Regardless of what would happen next, at that moment, I was proud.

Rule #1: Establish a Vision

You need to know your end goal before you can start crafting a strategy. Less than two hours after walking out of that meeting, I received an email granting us full approval to move forward with the project. Let's put this in perspective. Congressman Conyers was the Dean of Congress, which means he was the highest-ranked member of the House of Representatives. He was also the highest-ranked member of the Judiciary Committee and Congressional Black Caucus. When I received the official approval shortly after our meeting, my sense of pride quickly shifted to responsibility. From that moment, it was game on.

Rule #2: Establish Roles

Before my partner and I parted that afternoon, we established our roles. We clearly defined each person's responsibilities. Anything related to selecting a sculptor was all him. My role was essentially to manage the project, maintain a positive relationship with the congressman's office, and manage the media and marketing. Things were going great. But I neglected one key element when working in a team environment. I didn't sign a contract. This lesson is essential to your growth and development. Until you learn it, you will find yourself falling into similar situations over and over again. Here's how the project ended.

My partner did a phenomenal job locating a sculptor. We went through a few potential candidates before settling on Mr. Steven Whyte of Carmel, California. His work was simply breathtaking. While that was going on across the country, I was working to see if we could get this sculpture in the Smithsonian. My original goal was to try to have it appear as part of the grand opening for the African-American Museum of History and Culture in September of 2016, but when I learned it was too late to be considered, my partner and I started engaging in conversations with the National Portrait Gallery. I was simultaneously working to see if we could have an unveiling of the bust during The Congressional Black Caucus (CBC) in September 2016, as well. As fate would have it, one of my clients rented the Carnegie Library, which sits directly across the street from the Washington Convention Center, where the main sessions for The Congressional Black Caucus take place. Everything was aligning. For the big reveal, we had over one hundred attendees, and the Congressman and his team were so impressed that we hosted a separate reveal at Arena stage during the Michigan party during CBC.

Rule #3: Complete the Mission

The success of the unveiling celebration pushed me that much harder to find a way to have the work of art appear in the Smithsonian. The Monday following the Caucus events, I reached back out to the National Portrait Gallery to let them know how overjoyed Congressman Conyers was when he laid eyes on the bronze bust for the first time. It was then that she let me know that the review board would be accepting potential pieces to evaluate in a few short weeks. Of course, this was just what I wanted to hear. With excitement, I shared the news with my teammate only to learn that the podium that housed the bust ended up damaged during its time in DC. Now, we had a finite amount of time to get the bust remounted, packaged, and shipped back across the country before the review period.

Things were starting to get quite shaky between my partner and me during this period, but I stayed the course. I didn't allow emotion and personal issues to deter me from completing the mission. Often times, when you're being tried and tested, you must remember your why. If you lose sight of why you're compelled to do the work you're tackling, you can easily become distracted and lose focus. Maintaining a strong sense of why will give you the strength you need to continue pushing forward, no matter the adversities.

Because we were only in the first round of evaluations, I was able to submit professional quality images for the board's initial review. A few weeks later, I learned that the piece my partner commissioned had made it to the second round of evaluations, which required us to have the museum pick the bust up from a local location. By this point, communication between my partner and me was pretty much null and void. I had to send messages through the sculptor and all kinds of other shenanigans went on until the job was done. I can honestly say that working on that project taught me a lot about partnerships, relationships, and life. But when I received an official notice that the Smithsonian National Portrait Gallery would be installing the bronze bust of Congressman John J. Conyers, Jr. into the Smithsonian, I didn't care about anything else. I just wanted to call the Congressman myself and say, "Mission accomplished."

I'm not certain if former Congressman Conyers ever got to see the sculpture in the Smithsonian National Portrait Gallery, but I'm grateful that I was able to be a part of his story before he died October 27, 2019.

Throughout your life, I'm certain you've had to tap into that still small voice inside of you to make some powerful solutions manifest. Well, that's the same thing that I want you to do for your business. It's amazing what you can accomplish when your mind is clear and you have direct access to channeling your inner purpose. It's so unfortunate to walk into a room and ask the audience if they feel as though they're walking in their purpose and over half of the room is uncertain. Allow me to ask you: do you know what your purpose is? There are a number of different ways to tap into what your purpose is. I always tell people that passion and purpose tend to intersect when you're operating within your sweet spot. Your sweet spot means you are utilizing your innate gifts and leaning on source for guidance and, most importantly, for answers.

Don't allow your mind to tell you you're not ready. It's okay if you've never had formal training in business. Most of us haven't. The difference is, when the discomfort occurs, will you lean into it (to push through) or will you turn away because it's too much? Most successful people lean into the process because they trust it.

I recently spoke with my girlfriend's husband about his desire to join her small business by adding his capabilities to her business offerings. However, shortly after he shared his desire to work alongside his wife, he started making excuses like, "I don't know how many potential clients will be interested in the service offerings that I want to provide," and "I don't know how to market this new department to her existing clientele." You see, comfort and complacency are no good for the successful business owner. It's time to replace the negative thoughts with positive actions.

There's a difference between having a legit business idea with a clear business structure that addresses the needs of others and self-absorbed "get rich money schemes." You have to be able to decipher between the two. Your business idea can't be an ego booster that isn't beneficial to someone else. A sound business idea addresses the needs of others, while also enhancing the lives of others. Does your idea do that? If so, remember to rely on your inner strength and shift your mindset before you launch the business. If you walk into your business hesitant and teetering between fear and assurance, the energy around your business will be confused. Allow your inner thoughts to attract the ideal clients, and the positive forces that the universe can send your way, accept because you're owning the vision and embracing the journey.

CHAPTER 5:

Execute—Plan Like A Boss

"There is no secret to success.
It is the result of preparation, hard work, and
learning from failure."
– Colin Powell

have a friend who runs her hair salon out of her home. She can compete with any of the stylists in the big brand salons, but she decided to use her home as her workspace. If she ever decided to transition into a full-time entrepreneur, she would need to start from scratch to get the business legitimately established. Where would she begin? If you're in a similar predicament or even if you have fewer liabilities, this chapter will equip you with the basic know-how to get you headed in the right direction. I'm no lawyer. You'll want to check your jurisdiction to ensure that all of your state's requirements are met to avoid any penalties or fees.

Let's start with having a lawyer. A number of people are averse to paying those astronomical lawyer fees, but the truth of the matter is that if you invest from the beginning, it will save you in the long run. Why would you need a lawyer, you might ask? Well, they can work with you to ensure you have selected the proper business designation, namely a sole proprietorship, LLC, s-corp, corporation, or nonprofit. They can also assist you with drafting contracts for your clients. My lawyer is amazing; I use RJ Maples and Associates, a woman-owned firm out of New York that assists me with drafting all of my major contracts. The great part about it is that, once it's done, you can tweak the language or change the recipients based on the contract.

Again, I'm not a lawyer. You should consult with your lawyer before modifying the documents they provide. Your attorney is also an amazing sounding board if you're considering selling your company. You need to know all of the facts. Trust me, unless law is your specialty—and business law, at that—then you should not attempt to decipher lawyer lingo. It's just not a good use of your time. If you are in real estate, don't attempt to get counsel about tax law from your friend who is in family law. You want someone who can confidently assist you and represent you. Don't be afraid to interview a few firms to find the perfect match for you and your brand.

When you decide to register your business name with your state or receive your Articles of Incorporation, there is typically a nominal fee. One of my favorite stages of establishing a business entails cross-checking the existing business names to ensure my company's name is distinguishable. I'll tell you a little secret. Before I register a business, I also cross-check available domain names, which are website URLs, to ensure that my brand can be cohesive. I typically take it a step further and check social media handles on all platforms so my brand can have a uniform strategy from the beginning. We'll dive into this a lot more in Chapter 6, but since you're learning about structure, I figured I'd share how I typically go about selecting my company name. If that seems daunting to you, it shouldn't.

I'm sure you probably have a couple business names floating around in your head, but you probably have a favorite one. Here's another little secret. Your business doesn't necessarily have to be incorporated in the state where you live. A number of people establish businesses in states that don't have business taxes, such as Delaware or Nevada. But, if you go that route, remember that your business is subject to the laws of the state that you establish the business in. One additional requirement is that you will need a resident agent, a third-party who is located in the same state of a business entity who has been granted permission to receive correspondence from the Secretary of State, service of process notices, and other official government notices.

To give you an example, I live in the DC metropolitan area. There are three states within ten minutes of each other. If I wanted to start a nonprofit in Virginia but there's a business with the exact name as the business I want to start, I can check the Maryland state website to see if the name is available there. Pretty cool, huh? So, don't give up on establishing your business and giving it the perfect name. Just be sure to check its name availability in other places where you don't mind establishing your brand.

All right. Now that the business has it's Articles of Incorporation—or sometimes called Articles of Organization—you'll want to visit the official IRS site to register your business and to acquire an Employer Identification Number (EIN). This is an important step because, without it, you can't establish a business bank account, pay your taxes, or be officially considered a business. You'll want to take your time in applying. When you get to this point, you'll need to know the type of business you are planning to establish:

Sole Proprietorship

(I don't recommend this one because it's tied to your social security number)

Pros

- Easy to start up (no need to register your business with the state).
- No corporate formalities or paperwork requirements, such as meeting minutes, bylaws, etc.
- You can deduct most business losses on your personal tax return.

- Tax filing is easy—simply fill out and attach Schedule C-Profit or Loss From Business to your personal income tax return.

Cons

- As the only owner, you're personally liable for all of the business's debts and liabilities—someone who wins a lawsuit against your business can take your personal assets (your car, personal bank accounts, even your home in some situations).
- There's no real separation between you and the business, so it's more difficult to get a business loan and raise money (lenders and investors prefer LLCs or Corps).
- It's harder to build business credit without a registered business entity.

Partnership

Pros

- Easy to start up (no need to register your business with the state).
- No corporate formalities or paperwork requirements, such as meeting minutes, bylaws, etc.
- You don't need to absorb all the business losses on your own because the partners divide the profits and losses.
- Owners can deduct most business losses on their personal tax returns.

Cons

- Each owner is personally liable for the business's debts and other liabilities.
- In some states, each partner may be personally liable for another partner's negligent actions or behavior (this is called joint and several liability).
- Disputes among partners can unravel the business (though drafting a solid partnership agreement can help you avoid this).
- It's more difficult to get a business loan, land a big client, and build business credit without a registered business entity.

Limited Liability Company (LLC)

Pros

- Owners don't have personal liability for the business's debts or liabilities.
- You can choose whether you want your LLC to be taxed as a partnership or as a corporation.
- Not as many corporate formalities compared to an S-Corp or C-Corp.

Cons

- It's more expensive to create an LLC than a sole proprietorship or partnership (requires registration with the state).

Corporation

Pros

- Owners (shareholders) don't have personal liability for the business's debts and liabilities.
- C-corporations are eligible for more tax deductions than any other type of business.
- C-corporation owners pay lower self-employment taxes.
- You have the ability to offer stock options, which can help you raise money in the future.

Cons

- More expensive to create than sole proprietorships and partnerships (filing fees range from $100 to $500 based on which state you're in).
- C-corporations face double taxation: The company pays taxes on the corporate tax return, and then shareholders pay taxes on dividends on their personal tax returns.
- Owners cannot deduct business losses on their personal tax return.
- There are a lot of formalities that corporations have to meet, such as holding board meetings and shareholder meetings, keeping meeting minutes, and creating bylaws.

S-Corporation (S-Corp)

Pros
- Owners (shareholders) don't have personal liability for the business's debts and liabilities.
- No corporate taxation and no double taxation: An S-Corp is a pass-through entity, so the government taxes it much like a sole proprietorship or partnership.

Cons
- Like C-corporations, S-corporations are more expensive to create than both sole proprietorships and partnerships (requires registration with the state).
- There are more limits on issuing stock in S-corps versus C-Corps.
- You still need to comply with corporate formalities, like creating bylaws and holding board and shareholder meetings.

Registering for an EIN is completely free, and at the end of the registration process, you can download your EIN letter immediately, in most cases.

After I have these two documents, I essentially feel official. However, you need to cross-check the district or county laws to determine if you have to register for a business license, or if you are doing business under any other names besides your official business name. Then, you'll want to complete a "doing business as" form, which typically has a nominal fee associated with the filing.

Once you're straight with ensuring the government gets their money and the state has provided you a business name, you should purchase business insurance. I know it sounds like another massive cost, but it's pretty insignificant when you think of the protection it provides your business. Most corporate clients require that you have some form of business insurance, and some may even ask to be added to your policy (no additional fee and common). It's worth the investment to figure out the best business insurance firm for your company. For most industries, general liability might be all you need. Because I speak a lot publicly, I also carry an errors and omissions policy to protect what might and might not come out of my mouth. Do your research and figure out what is best for you and your business.

When you begin hiring employees, many states will require you to have a workman's compensation policy as well, which protects employees if they get hurt on the job. I'm not going to go deep into that, as there are a number of required policies, but I wanted to at least provide you a brief introduction to some of the structural requirements you'll need to ensure you are up to date with for your business and elements you'll want to get established.

A lot has been covered. Of course, there is plenty more to look at, but first, let's take a step back and talk about establishing a business bank account. For many of you who have been in business independently, you've probably married your personal monies with your company's revenue. When you decide to build out your small business, I'm going to encourage you to kill that practice. How will you show the company's profit and losses at the end of the year? You'll want to determine a certain salary for yourself and pay that amount to yourself every month. Additional money that the company makes should go in your business account. What this does is set the tone for how you'll pay for all of your business needs. You shouldn't have to pay for business expenses out of your personal account. Trust me. Get in the habit of practicing this early; it will save you priceless time during tax season.

Speaking of taxes, I am an advocate for letting people perform the tasks they specialize in. An accountant, bookkeeper, or CPA are worth the investment to me. If you are good with budgets and filing your taxes, this might be easy-breezy for you. For me, it would take forever and a year to get my taxes filed probably, more so out of fear of doing something wrong, but either way, make sure you're utilizing a tool to help you keep your financial business in order. Even though I utilize a CPA, I manage the everyday invoicing via an online financial management platform. There are a lot of different ones. Some are free and others come with a monthly cost. Figure out which one will work best for you, and get it set up so you can easily see monies coming in and going out.

Once all of your business necessities are in place, it's time to start the business-planning phase. For the sake of highlighting the importance of a business plan, we're going to introduce you to an abbreviate version, or a one-sheet business plan. I am the queen of brevity, therefore I love the idea of mapping out your annual strategy. If you have a vision in mind, start there, have a plan in place, and work your way out. Even the Bible says to, "Write the vision, make it plain" (Habakkuk 2:2 ESV). I believe there is power in transferring your ideas from your mind to paper. It makes it real, and you can better hold yourself accountable. Below are my top three necessities for your one-sheet plan?

Identify who your target audience is. If you don't have a vision statement or even a business name, you have to know whom your products or services are targeted. You need to be able to clearly articulate who needs your products or services? If you have a great idea but no one is in need of what you want to offer, the idea is pretty much dead. Before you go wasting time, energy, or money have a clear understanding of who you're going to be servicing.

How do you plan to make money from your business? What problem are you solving for your customer? Is your product or service offering something people are willing to pay money for? In the next chapter, we'll dive into this more. But you want to make sure you're bringing something unique to the table that adds value to your target audience.

How do you plan to reach your target audience? Nowadays, most people automatically throw out social media as their solution when attempting to reach their target demographic. The truth of the matter is not everyone buys products and services from social media. You have to conduct a little market research to have a better understanding of your target audience's behaviors. You should know how they buy, where they're currently purchasing, who your competitors are, and most importantly, what makes you different. How are you going to convert them into paying clients for your business?

There are more things to include as part of your business plan, but those are my top three to get you started. You've got the business structure underway, but have you determined where you're going to run your business? Earlier in the chapter, you learned the benefits of registering your business in a remote location. Just remember you'll need a business address to do so. And, fortunately for you, remote offices are easy to find, and they can be pretty cost-effective. Most people have heard of WeWork. It's a pretty common shared workspace venue. With their membership, you have access to any of their other locations across the country. Similarly, there is a venue called Carr Workspaces. Carr Workplaces have packages to fit every budget. Whether you just need a space to collect your mail and answer your company's phone, or you want a dedicated office for your business, there are various options available to you.

When I first started my business, I utilized a P.O. box as my first business address. I purchased the service for a year, and I loved it. Mainly because instead of merely having a P.O. box, the post office provided me their address as my mailing address and the box number appeared as a suite number. It was perfect for my start-up budget and to the outside world, it appeared as a legit business location. For some of you, you might decide that using your house address will suffice, that's cool too. Just remember that it will be listed in most search results as your business address, as it's tied to your business registration with the state.

Lastly, I'd like to share another registration that most people rarely consider—registering your company to do business with the federal government. This is another free platform for you to set-up your business for success. The federal government has a trillion-dollar budget that most small businesses don't consider tapping into when they first launch their businesses. But, why not? To register, visit www.sam.gov. This is the official site to register for eligibility to be awarded a federal contract with the government. SAM stands for System for Awards Management.

Please be certain that the ending of the website that you visit is dot gov. I warn you because there are a number of "fake" sites in existence that will attempt to charge you to register your business with the government. While their service offerings might be valid, you have the ability to completely register your business at no cost. You will want to dedicate at least an hour to complete your account registration, but if you can't set aside a straight hour, you will have the opportunity to save your set-up and complete it at a later time.

Going back to your one sheet business plan, remember the first thing that I said was most important? Knowing your target audience. If you know the federal government is part of your ideal audience, you'll want to be sure to register your business in SAM to avoid delays when you start winning your big contracts. Yes, I'm already claiming that for you.

Throughout this chapter, a lot has been touched on. So much so that I'm going to recap some of the elements. The chapter started by discussing the various company structures for your business, whether you choose an LLC, a Corporation, or an S-Corp, you'll want to register your business with your state to obtain your Articles of Incorporation. Remember, each state might call this document something slightly different, but it's the official registration document of your new business. Then, you'll want to be sure to register your business with the Internal Revenue Service's office. You don't have to go into an IRS facility, you can complete this task one hundred percent online, and it's completely free. Again, you'll want to be sure that you're on a .gov website to ensure that you're on the correct site. I'd hate to call the other sites scam sites, but most will ask you a ton of questions and then attempt to charge you for services you don't need. You can complete the EIN registration without their assistance.

Then, I shared my top three elements for you to include in your one sheet business plan. Don't let my suggestion of completing a simple one-sheet plan deter you from completing a detailed business plan. I have merely abbreviated the process for those who are less likely to complete the full plan before moving to the next level.

But it's recommended that you evaluate all aspects of your business and complete a deep dive assessment at some point in your business life span.

I also discussed the importance of establishing a business bank account. The one thing I failed to mention earlier is to be sure that you take your time when selecting a bank. All banks are not created equally. Do your research. If you know you might need to apply for a loan, find out which banks are known for granting loans to small businesses. Check out the banks that are recognized by the U.S. Small Business Administration. If you are interested in government contracting, there are banks that understand the needs of businesses that target the government as their clients. Don't just hop into bed with a bank. Gain a complete understanding of all of their service offerings. Will they come out to your office to have documents notarized for you? Does your bank charge a notary fee? If you know that having wire transfers will be an essential element to your business, does the bank offer a remote wire transfer option to save you time from going into the bank? Will your business account be charged for certified checks or cashier checks? These are all elements to consider, and most people don't. This is the one union you'll want to make sure is strong. You want to establish a relationship with a bank that's mutually beneficial, not one-sided.

You now have an understanding of utilizing remote office locations. Determine the best option for you to establish your business. Will it be your home or a coworking space? Whatever option you choose, be sure that it aligns with your budget and the needs of your business.

Last but not least, you'll want to register your business to do business with the federal government on SAM. I am a huge supporter of small businesses doing business with the government, whether it's at the local, state, or federal level. It often feels like people are ill-informed about the needs of the government, therefore they don't seek the government as a potential client. I encourage you to include the government as part of your marketing strategy.

CHAPTER 6:

Account— Mind Your Business

"I feel that luck is preparation meeting opportunity."
— OPRAH WINFREY

Have you noticed your personal spending behaviors? Let's say you're at a farmer's market and, like most farmers markets, the vendors sell similar foods. If the quality of the food is equivalent and the price is the same, how do you decide who gets your money? Most of the time, it's the business with better customer engagement.

Now, let's say they have similar products and one vendor's prices are slightly higher. The vendor with the lower prices is rude and disrespectful, while the other is friendly and courteous. Which vendor would you be most inclined to patronage? Most people would probably say, "well I'm going to spend at the location with the better prices if the products are of the same quality," while other people, like me, won't spend money where it's not appreciated. The moral of the story is that most people opt to do business with people they like and those who make them feel appreciated.

As a business owner, you have to hold yourself to the same level of accountability. You have to remember the things that make you feel good about spending your money. Those same expectations you place on other businesses you support, you need to make sure that you're incorporating similar practices within your business. How do you do that? Throughout this chapter, you'll learn some key accountability markers to ensure that your business approach is strategically sound. We'll look at how you handle your financial projections, craft your marketing and brand strategy, as well as do a deeper dive into understanding your target market. So, grab your B.E.A.S.T. Mentality notebook, and let's get to it.

As you begin to flesh out the culture of your business—you have to decide what the brand experience looks like for your clients. Even if that brand experience is only executed by you (at the moment)—you need to determine what the key indicators are for your brand. What is the voice of the brand, what is the tone of the brand, and—most importantly—how do you make your clients feel?

To ensure that you're setting your team up for success, I recommend establishing standard operating procedures and an employee handbook. These two guides will serve as the reinforcement you need to implement structure and to successfully govern the culture of your business. Let's go through both of these documents to ensure you understand why they're important and what's incorporated in both.

Your standard operating procedures (SOP) should be combined into a single manual that lists instructions, step-by-step, on how to complete a task or handle a specific situation in the workplace. Here are my top four suggestions for developing your SOPs.

Step 1. Determine the key procedures you want your team to have structure around (i.e., newsletter format, use of logo, defusing conflict, etc.). Once you identify what those items are, create an outline that covers all of the tasks that you want to build out procedures for. The outline will act as your guide when the time comes to begin drafting the manual.

Step 2. Clearly articulate the purpose of the standard operating procedure manual and how it's expected to be implemented in the employees' (or contractors') work.

Step 3. Complete one task at a time from your outline (step 1). Provide the step-by-step process for completing the identified task. List the first task. Followed by a detailed explanation for executing the task. Make sure each step is clear and concise, but provide enough detail that anyone can follow the instructions.

Step 4. Give the standard operating procedure to someone else to read. Have an employee or someone you know read through and complete the instructions. They can provide valuable feedback if there are steps they could not complete or did not understand.

The other essential handbook for your company is your employee handbook. A good handbook should reflect your company culture, while also outlining clear and easy to understand company policies. Here are five reasons why your employee handbook is essential to your organization:

1. Set the tone in your workplace.
2. Communicate what is expected of employees.
3. Ensure your policies are clearly communicated.
4. Defend yourself against employee claims.
5. Explain your benefits and what sets you apart.

If you want to implement dress codes or tardy policies—this is the place for you to outline the expected and required behaviors at your business. If you fail to establish these guidebooks, your team will have no direction on what's acceptable and tolerable behavior. If you take the time to outline clear expectations, your team won't have anything to dispute.

In phase two of your B.E.A.S.T. Mentality program, you learned about identifying your target audience. When you're working to identify who your target market is, you have to know exactly what it is that you're selling. Once upon a time, I worked for AARP, a nonprofit organization that's dedicated to all things seniors. They want people to live better and longer, and they provide resources to help individuals succeed at every stage of "aging." One thing I've always admired about the organization is that they know their target markets inside and out. Here's how strategic they are. AARP The Magazine is one of the most highly distributed magazines in the country. Instead of creating one magazine for the fifty-year-old and older population, which is their target market, they break each magazine down by decade. The fifty to fifty-nine-year-olds have one magazine, the sixty to sixty-nine-year-olds have theirs, and so on and so forth. This is what I call knowing your audience and marketing directly to their specific needs.

If I stick with the example above, in the magazine for the fifty to fifty-nine-year-olds, AARP might be selling information about preparing for retirement and saving for retirement travel. In the seventy to seventy-nine magazine, I'm certain they're not discussing planning for retirement, as that wouldn't necessarily be relevant information for that audience. Before you can market effectively, you have to know what it is that you're hoping to put in the hands of your clients. It's also necessary to know where your market is currently buying the services you provide and they need.

If you have a yoga business and you're looking to attract more pregnant women to take classes at your studio, are you going to promote your business at the hottest nightclub in the city? No, because the majority of your target audience isn't at the club. Now, that's not to say that no pregnant women frequent clubs, it's just saying that it's not the main venue for you to spend money to market your business. Take your time when you research who your client is. It's great to think of one person that you're looking to help with your product or service. Determine how this product or service will change their life, and that's what you structure your marketing around. Always keep in mind that you are here to market how your product or service will benefit your client—they don't care what it's called (within reason). However, they will purchase if they understand how it makes their lives better. You'll want to know their age, sex, career level, and possibly their hobbies. When you know exactly who your target market is, then you're ready to start marketing to them.

Marketing Intro

You're now ready to craft your marketing strategy. Your marketing strategy essentially entails your plan for touching or reaching your customers. Before you begin working on your outward engagement, I want you to dial it back some to focus on your internal brand. Before you can tell the world who you are, you must have a complete understanding of your business. With that being said, you need to have a clear understanding of your brand messaging. Here are some essential elements to examine.

Logo

By now, you should have a company name, but what does it look like? How does it make a person feel? These are all things you should consider when crafting your company logo. You should look up color psychology to understand how certain colors make people feel. For instance, did you know that most airplanes use blue seat cushions because blue has a calming effect? It's quite interesting. I challenge you to do a little research before you build your logo. You could just select your favorite colors, or you can gain a better understanding of how colors cause a reaction in the brain and decide what are the best colors to draw people into your businesses.

Tagline

If I say, "Just do it." or, "I'm lovin' it," I don't need to say anything else for you to know exactly what I'm talking about. Both Nike and McDonald's have done an amazing job training us to think of their brands when you hear the three words from their slogan. Your challenge will be to create a short, catchy slogan that will resonate with your target audience. Your tagline should not exceed eight words. Remember that it's a supportive phrase to complement your company's name.

Vision

What is the overarching vision you have for your company? Why are you starting this company? What need do you hope it will service? These are all questions I want you to think about as you craft your vision statement. It shouldn't just be for your company. It should also reflect how, through your successful implementation of your mission, it will make the community and world better. Remember the person that you thought about when you were drafting who your target audience is? Well, think of that person as you craft your vision for your company. It doesn't have to be complicated, check out the Alzheimer's Associations Vision Statement: "A world without Alzheimer's disease." It's concise, yet it answers all of the questions needed to have a strong vision statement.

Mission

Think back to the why statement that you created under the first step for the B.E.A.S.T. Mentality program; now I want you to create a "why" for your company. Your mission statement is essentially your road map to executing your vision statement. What's your path to get there? Here's the Alzheimer's Association's Mission Statement, just so you can see how they work together: "To eliminate Alzheimer's disease through the advancement of research; to provide and enhance care and support for all affected; and to reduce the risk of dementia through the promotion of brain health."

Do you see how the two work in tandem? If you already have a vision and mission statement for your business, please take some time to ensure that they're in alignment with the strategy outlined above. These two elements might seem simple and pointless, but they are the elements that will keep you on track to fulfilling the goals of your organization.

Now that you have these elements, you're ready to start working on your forward promotion or external marketing materials. Here are the most immediate suggestions to get you started:

Business Card

These days, there are so many options for making your cards stand out. Depending on your industry, you can spend a lot of money here, or you can be "green" and economical and get away with an electronic business card. You have to decide the feel of your company and ensure it is reflected consistently through your marketing materials. The industry of your business also plays a significant role in the presentation of your business card. For instance, if you have a landscaping business, you might utilize a real image (of a project that your company executed) on your business card. I would go as far as to highlight that the image is from an actual client. This is an element that will serve as a differentiator. You're showing potential clients immediately the quality of your work. They don't have to visit your website to see examples. You're saving them time by showcasing your skills immediately.

Now, if your clientele is primarily the government, I would suggest incorporating your NAICS codes on your business card. What are NAICS codes? They are identifiers the government uses to categorize services. It's not uncommon to see a company's top five service offerings on the back of their business card. I would also include any designations your company might have (i.e., economically disadvantaged woman-owned business, veteran-owned, HUBZone, etc.). These are all key elements that can stand out to potential partners and contract officers.

Because your business card typically serves as the first tangible marketing document that you distribute, I'm going to provide one last example. If you offer a product or service that requires a consultation or a discovery call prior to determining if someone is a good fit for your services, I recommend having a direct link to your calendar available on your card. There are a number of scheduling applications on the market, so select the one that works best for you and your budget (and yes, some are free). I also recommend including your social media handle on your business card. This is a great way to build up your follower base while also highlighting the work of your brand.

Your One Sheet

Your one sheet can vary drastically depending on your industry. But at the end of the day, it is essentially a sheet that provides information on the following: who you are, service offerings, differentiators, past performance, and contact information. These five topics are applicable for a marketing postcard or a capability statement for the government. This is one sheet of paper that provides the nuts and bolts of who you are and what you can do for your clients.

Professional Headshot of the Business Owner

This is usually the last thing people think about when it comes to marketing, but when it comes to your personal profile on LinkedIn, you should not have a selfie as your profile picture. You also want to be sure you have a professional headshot in the event you're asked to speak somewhere and they want to highlight you, or if you want to use it in your marketing materials. Remember what was said earlier—people do business with people they like. If you're a likable person, your picture might be a real selling point if it's incorporated into your marketing strategy.

Do Your Dollars Make Sense?

Do you know your worth? Unfortunately, when many business owners start out, they don't. If you're transitioning from corporate America doing the same type of work you were doing before, you might not know how to price your services. Most people don't take their previous salaries and divide it down to an hourly rate to figure it out, either—most make excuses for why they don't feel worthy to charge what they're worth. They'll tell themselves things like "no one is going to pay me that much money to do x, y or z" or "I have to work my way back up to the top." If you've never told yourself any of those things, congratulations, but for me, those are the things I believed too. I would volunteer my services just to get my name out, almost as if I were a newbie and I didn't know what I was doing.

Now, there is nothing wrong with volunteering your services or even performing some work at a discount to gain visibility. However, there needs to be a clear strategy for how you plan to transition from discount to full fee. If you don't know what that plan is, it's time to construct it. Otherwise you'll find yourself in a cycle of charging much less than your services are worth.

I can recall a time when I would have conversations with people and give away all types of free advice completely unintentionally. It wasn't until one day that I was out with my best friend and we were listening to a live band. Afterward, we went to eat with the performers. The pianist had asked me one simple question, and I went from zero to one hundred with providing him and his band members a plan for building out their business. To be honest, I don't even remember what all I told them, but I knew it was good because the members pulled out their phones and started taking notes. I clearly didn't mind because I just kept talking. My friend later pointed out to me that I had just given them probably thousands of dollars' worth of information for free. Again, me having such a servant's heart and wanting folks to win, it didn't bother me that I didn't feel consumed for not charging for my services. Honestly, I don't think it registered what was happening during that moment. It wasn't until I got in a situation where my bills were due that I realized the disservice I had been providing myself. I don't want you to start off charging below your worth. You have to always remember who you are and the value you're going to bring into your clients' lives. Don't be afraid to step out on faith and own who you are. Trust me, you're worth every penny—I know I am. Don't price yourself out of business.

Back in 2018, I interviewed one of the most brilliant millennial financial literacy experts I know. Ms. Dominique Broadway joined me on The Woman Behind the Business Talk Show on our episode titled "Mind Your

Money, Grow Your Business." She dropped some powerful nuggets around taking control of your business financials. In a nutshell, she advises clients to work backwards.

What does that mean? Well, in order for you to determine how you'll meet your annual revenue goals, you'll first need to identify your targeted revenue goal. You'll want to figure out all of your anticipated service offerings for the year. Then you'll break down various projections by month. The easiest way to do it entails creating a chart that houses all of your services, and then you'll come up with as many combinations as you can to reach your desired annual salary.

Let's say you provide social media marketing services, and your prices range from $500 to $2,500 a month, and your projected annual revenue is $100,000, then you would work backward to determine how many of each package you would need to sell per month to reach your annual goals. It's not a difficult task, however it is one ingredient that most new CEO's fail to set aside time to execute.

Pricing

Most people are so afraid to sell, but the reality is everyone is a salesperson. The successful people tend to embrace their ability to sell, while others hide from it. Stop hiding.

If you believe in the services you're providing, you should be able to proudly announce your rate with confidence and assurance. There should be no hesitation, and if people sense uncertainty, they won't bite. They'll shop around. If your confidence screams, "You need me," they'll feel it. They'll believe that they do need you.

Lastly, you have to be consistent with your pricing. Determine a rate and stick to it. In the Support Module of B.E.A.S.T. Mentality, you're going to hear some pretty nasty truths regarding how family and friends won't necessarily want to support your business. They'll be looking to you with great expectancy of free or discounted items. You'll want to nip that in the bud before it becomes a problem. If you want to have a standard friends and family discount, then you need to factor that into your pricing projections before the question is ever asked. You can also establish a brand ambassador program where you provide so many complimentary or discounted items to individuals who will be tasked with building your brand. But, as I stated, this needs to be planned out thoroughly, with your annual financial goal in mind. And please learn the word, "No." The sooner you can own your ability to tell family and friends "no," the closer you'll be to reaching your bottom line successfully every year.

I remember meeting the head of fundraising for the Smithsonian and asking her how she handles asking people for money. Her response was priceless. She said, "I don't look at it as if I'm merely asking for money. I look at it as though I'm providing the individual with the opportunity to be a part of something great." If you look at your service offerings as an opportunity for your prospective clients to be aligned with greatness, then you should have no qualms about selling.

I can't stress the importance of managing your financials enough. You have the power to make as much or as little as you want. If your pricing is in alignment with your competitors and your marketing plan is clear, you are structuring your business for success. You are laying down all of the necessary groundwork to walk away from your corporate career and lean into your full-time business.

By the end of this book, you will have all of the necessary resources to jumpstart your journey into full-time entrepreneurship. With every page, you should be gaining confidence that making the transition is possible. This isn't something you have to go through alone. I love helping clients reach their full potential as entrepreneurs. I know you can do this, you just have to decide that you're ready.

CHAPTER 7:

Support—Build Your Village

"You can make more friends in two months by becoming interested in other people than you can in two years by trying to get other people interested in you."
– DALE CARNEGIE

Who's in your village? Is it your mom, sister, girlfriend, husband, wife, or a compilation of friends and family? This question is important because these are the people you hold in high enough regard to assist you with your business. While they might not be intricate workers or even hold a position in the company, they are your sounding board and your most trusted sources. You should have people in your "village" or trusted circle who you know will have your back when times get hard. The funny thing about your village is sometimes it's made up of people you never thought would make it into such a prestigious place in your life.

I use the phrase village because most of us have heard the phrase, "It takes a village to raise a child." Well, I believe it takes a village to be successful. This village is typically made up of mentors, friends, family, and your team of workers. Throughout this chapter, you will discover the good, the bad, and the "kick this person out of the village," scenarios to help you ensure you have the support system you need to be successful.

Let's start with mentors. I have come across a number of individuals who are afraid of the word mentor. I'm not sure if they're scared of something being revealed about themselves to someone else, or if the phrase is just so "above" them that it makes them uncomfortable. A mentor is merely a trusted resource that you can learn from, brainstorm your ideas with, and essentially they're there to help position you for success.

When I first started my business, DC Media Connection, I knew I needed to surround myself with successful men and women. Don't miss that, because it's essential to your success. You shouldn't just have mentors who look like you, in the same industry as you, at the same level as you. Your mentor should be someone who is doing something in an industry in which you have interest so they can provide you with insights, information, and inspiration.

I've honestly been blessed to have a number of amazing mentors strategically positioned in my life. These are people I know were ordained to provide me guidance and to prepare me for where I am at this moment. However, my first mentor as a business owner was well versed in government contracting and, at the time, had been in business for nearly fifteen years. What attracted me most to her was she had clearly built a multimillion-dollar cybersecurity company that catered to the government as her main source of revenue. At the time, I knew nothing about the government contracting space. I wanted her as a mentor because she could provide me with insight into something in which I had zero experience. My second mentor was someone in a similar industry to mine. She had built up a powerful reputation and was clearly at a level in her career I aspired to reach. So, deciding to ask her was a no-brainer.

The last mentor that I will share with you is an international business genius. He works for a company that creates treaties with international territories and is just a great resource for international business. When I started DC Media Connection, I had no idea I would eventually end up with international clients. However, I had positioned myself to have access to resources and information, so when opportunities surfaced, I wasn't scrambling for help.

You're probably wondering, "okay this sounds good, but what do you say to someone who you want to be your mentor?" Well, it's pretty simple, actually. You tell them exactly what your ask is. If you have just met the person, you don't have to ask them on the spot. If they don't know anything about you, that could be a little weird. Instead, greet them, spark up a conversation, and then ask if they might be available for you to treat them to coffee, tea, or an after-work happy hour.

Again, that's another important tip—you should make it known that you are planning to pay for their time by treating them to connect. If your potential mentor is anything like me, they're not interested in setting aside time to meet you somewhere, give free information, and then have to pay for the experience, unless it's placed on their heart to do so.

Once you connect with your potential mentor, take your time with the conversation; don't just jump into what it is that you want. Show them that you have genuine interest in who they are, what they've accomplished with their work, etc. In order to do this, you're going to have to do a little research about the person.

The worse feeling in the world is having someone meet up with you and it's clear that they just want to talk about themselves and what they want. The sooner that you learn how to remove yourself as the priority, the sooner people will see your value.

Then, once you've shared what you admire about them, wait for them to say something along the lines of "well, tell me a little more about you." If they don't ask, you should still be able to easily transition the conversation by saying something like: "Because of all of the amazing achievements you've been able to accomplish, I wanted to know if you might be someone I can call on if I need advice from time to time."

Please don't ask if you can pick their brain. For some individuals, it can come across as you using them for free information. Now, asking if you can reach out for advice is also soliciting free information, but it's direct. You're clearly articulating what your intentions are. If the potential mentor agrees to allow you to reach out, do not become a nuisance, respect their time, and allow the relationship to grow organically. I promise it will with time and persistence. If they say no, that's okay, too. Or they have too many mentees already. Or they just might not think that you're a good fit for their style of mentoring. Either way, don't let it deter you—there is someone waiting to be the perfect mentor to you.

Here's another hidden secret, when you learn how to network effectively, which you'll learn how to do later in this chapter, you will be able to email people you've met over the years and just run questions by them. Trust me, some of my mentors don't even know I consider them a mentor. Remember, a mentor is just a trusted advisor.

You've learned how to select a mentor and how to ask them to advise you. The next groups we'll tackle are friends and family. The friends and family category can be a little hard to swallow. I'll share some personal examples to hopefully share from a place of experience. Your friends and family members won't always be your number one supporters. Please grasp this concept now. It'll be easier to swallow when one, or most of them, don't meet your expectations.

It's not because they don't want to. It has more to do with capacity. Let me begin by saying this. Your vision is something God trusted you with. If God provided you a vision, he knows you're equipped to manifest it no matter how crazy it might seem. It was handcrafted for you. You have to realize early on that everyone isn't capable of receiving or understanding what God has trusted you with. Their capacity isn't on your level. That's not to say you're better than them or anything of the sort, but it is to let you know that some things are better kept to yourself. Allow your work to speak for what you're doing. This can alleviate a lot of pain in the long run. I have had a number of clients who felt completely deflated because their friends and family wouldn't support them. Support doesn't always come in the form of financial support. Emotional support is real, but here are a few ways you might classify not feeling supported:

- They only want free or discounted items.
- They don't show up to any of your events
- They never purchase your products or services
- They don't help with your business, even if it's as simple as sharing information that you're doing on their social media accounts
- They don't ask you about your business, but they'll ask for money

There are plenty more variations, but these are the big ones. If you've ever endured any of this with your side business, let me be the first to tell you it doesn't get better when your business becomes your only source of income. The reality is, it just might get a little worse. I don't know what it is about our families' psyche, but for some reason when you tell people, "Oh, I own a business now," they think it automatically equates to, "Oh, I make a lot of money." Any real business owner knows that's not the case necessarily. Especially not when you're first starting out. I also want to warn you to protect your feelings. This can be one of the hardest parts of having a business. You will lose friends, and for some, you may become distant from your family. Why would this happen? Well, you begin to see who your real friends are. You will begin to associate with people differently, and it's okay. Everyone isn't equipped to handle your what's next. Understanding that everyone has a season in your life is essential. Don't allow expired relationships to drag down you or your business.

While I was married, my husband would tell me he wanted us to spend more time together, but he also put demands on me to bring home a certain amount of money. This was a huge tug-of-war for me. I told him that it wasn't that I didn't want to spend time together, it was just that I didn't want to waste time. Now, I wasn't saying that spending time with him would be a waste, but watching TV for an hour wasn't a priority to the goals I had set for myself. I felt like we could spend time doing something that would be productive for the business. I would have preferred to work in the house together, complete something business-related, or any activity that would check off something from our "to-do" checklist. Some people might say I should have just allocated the time to do a senseless deed that was important to him, but for whatever reason, I couldn't maintain it. I tried. I could have possibly tried a little harder, but unfortunately, it wasn't high on my priority list. You have to decide what is important to you and stick to it. All of your decisions won't be easy and everyone won't understand them, but at the end of the day, if you can live with those decisions, that's all that matters.

To counter the bad layers around support, you will have a small group of family and friends who will be your number one cheerleaders. These individuals will stay up with you until the wee hours of the morning to help you think through an idea. They'll pray with you and for you. They'll be your encouragers when you feel like giving up, and they'll be there to tell you when you're going off track. This small group of people will be your most valuable asset. Please be sure to take the time to take care of them and provide them with as much love and care as they provide you. For many of them, they won't require much, so, be sure to toss out a lot of thank yous, words of gratitude, and show how much you appreciate them through small gestures. It will keep them feeling appreciated. It will fuel them on days they need a few doses of encouragement.

It's now time to discuss your support staff. These are the individuals you decide to hire to assist you with building your business. For many of us, our first round of support staff members may be a combination of family and friends. There's nothing wrong with that, but it's essential to provide them with clear expectations and boundaries. One of my clients had hired her sister to assist her with vending her products at various trade shows. Her sister would arrive to work late at least one day a week, and most days, she knew when it would happen—the night after she would go out partying. She adjusted her schedule to make it easier on her sister and she'd still arrive late.

She grew frustrated because she needed someone who could be reliable to relieve her of needing to be onsite. She finally made the decision that it was best that they part ways. The mother got involved and made my client feel bad about firing her sister. I share this because it's important to consider what might happen if you have to release a family member; however, it is easier to do so if you have the proper training materials in place. It's imperative to the success of your business that you make the hard decisions. If one of your workers is not performing to the level you need them to, they gotta go. It's that simple, especially if you're paying them. I tell my clients to hire slow and fire fast. This is important if you have a team of people watching. If people think they can get away with things, they're going to do whatever they think they can get away with. You have to be in control of the culture of your company. One toxic person can shift the direction of the entire company quickly. You have to be strong enough to make an example out of that person to show what's tolerated and what's not. It's as simple as that. You also have to be willing to implement the repercussions for not following the employee handbook and your standard operating procedures.

Effective Networking

The number one thing most people miss when it comes to networking is being intentional with where they network. In the DC area on any given night, there might be over a hundred networking events. How do you decide which ones to attend? Some people gravitate toward the free events they come across on Eventbrite. Others will strategically place themselves at a bar at a popular hotel. Whatever you decide, have a strategy for where you're going. If you are going to the free networking event because your target market for clients would probably opt to go to a free event, then yes, that's where you need to be. But, if your clientele is high-end, you should not be at the free network after-work event. I'm not saying that there are no free events high-end clients will attend. I'm just saying be strategic with your time. Check different organizational calendars. They typically post their upcoming events, and networking naturally occurs after these events. Don't just sign up to go to every networking event across the city. Your time is money, and no one should be frivolously wasting it.

Now, that you know where you're going, you need to have a plan for how you show up. How you show up is incredibly important. That first impression is a priceless moment you can never get back. When you decide to step out to represent you and your company, the number one thing that's important is your presentation. Take the time to pull yourself together with great intention. I have a personal weakness for Christian Louboutin shoes. Most people know them as red bottoms. For the type of work that I do, I feel as though their shoes make a statement. They're a conversation starter, and to me, they're memorable. I am intentionally going to make sure that my presentation package is sealed with my Louboutins. For you, it might be a bow tie or pearls—find something that can become your statement piece.

Now that you've created the image or brand you want to portray for yourself, be consistent. This portrayal can't change every day. Determine your look and stick to it. Consistency is key to every aspect of your business. Now it's time to make contact. You should always have on hand either a hard business card or an electronic one. Either way, when you're given a business card, be sure to take notes on the back of their card to distinguish them.

Remember how you intentionally placed a statement piece or signature piece as part of your wardrobe? For most people, that's something that they would remember. You also want to be sure you follow-up. When you do, you will use something from your conversation as part of the subject line of the email. Let them know it was great meeting them at whatever place you met and that you would like to stay connected. If you'd prefer not to send an email, connecting on the business social networking site LinkedIn is also an acceptable means of following up with someone.

I often notice people when they are networking. They get a little weird with people who mention that they are in similar or the same industries. Stop getting weird over that. It's a beautiful thing. I think our brains have been programmed to think that everything is a competition and everyone is our competitor—please throw that mentality in the garbage if you want to be successful. Do you think Beyoncé is threatened by Shakira? No. Successful people know the power of collaboration. If you meet someone who is in a similar line of work, notate that on their card and tag that information in your customer relationship management tool, or CRM. Having someone who can potentially be a future collaborative partner is essential to building and growing your business.

When the government puts out RFPs most of the time, it's a lot of work for one small business to handle on their own. Being able to call on resources is an important lesson I hope you're learning.

CHAPTER 8:

Transparent— Walk in Your Truth

"You can only become great at something you are willing to sacrifice for."

– MAYA ANGELOU

A few years back, I decided to create a safe space for women entrepreneurs to experience a guiltless vacation that would provide them professional and personal development. It was perfect. I had it all planned out. We would host our first Woman Behind the Business Retreat in Nassau, Bahamas, for five days of transformational engagement and powerful sessions to inspire, ignite, and impact women globally. The same day that our retreat was supposed to begin, Hurricane Irene swept across the Bahamas. The week before the storm hit,

I carefully tracked the storm, because I knew I needed to make a decision regarding the trip soon. I probably didn't make a final call until the airlines announced they would allow travel dates to be modified. I worked with this awful travel company, and I felt like they used the storm to their advantage to charge us additional fees. But, I digress.

The hardest part of this situation wasn't the money, fortunately; it was being able to lead a group of approximately fifty women through how we were going to handle modifying the trip. I had to stay in constant communication with the ladies to let them know everything was under control. I was a complete wreck internally, but on the outside, I appeared collected and well organized. Sometimes the hardest step toward a solution is facing the realities of the situation head-on.

I put myself in their position. I knew I needed to be able to come back to the table with a complete plan in place regarding how I would move the event forward. I presented my group of travelers with potential dates to reschedule the retreat, and fortunately, ninety percent of registered attendees were still able to join us the weekend immediately following Thanksgiving. And that became our official retreat weekend for two consecutive years. That was probably one of the hardest situations I ever had to maneuver through; however, through it all, I remained optimistic and transparent with the women about what was happening. I had to put myself in their shoes and think about what I would have wanted to see happen, especially if I had invested a couple thousand dollars toward something. Transparency is what led me out of that situation stronger than I went in. And as you've learned in earlier chapters, through leaning into the process, the rescheduled event ended up being bigger and better.

For instance, the wife of the Prime Minister of the Commonwealth of the Bahamas was not able to attend on the September date. However, she joined us in November. Gospel recording artist Tasha Page-Lockheart was able to perform at our closing ceremony in November as well. You see, if transparency did not exist throughout the chaos, most people would have opted to just get their money back and would have not thought twice about it. But because they trusted me throughout the storm, they remained committed to the ultimate cause, which was attending the retreat.

This is just one of many examples of how transparency can carry you through adversity. Throughout the final phase of the B.E.A.S.T. Mentality method, you will see how transparency evokes trust, but before we move on, I'd like you to think of a situation where you had to trust someone or an organization through a difficult situation. Think about how the situation was handled. What did you agree with, and what did you not agree with? Did you opt to work with this person or company again after the encounter? Why or why not?

Most of the time, individuals in leadership deal with various obstacles. It's their character that often makes the difference in the outcome of the situation. Have you ever heard the quote, "Don't let your gift take you where your character can't keep you?" The first time I heard someone say this, I thought it was so profound. Many times, you are blessed with amazing gifts, and once you truly hone in and tap into the full capabilities of your innate gifts, you realize that you can accomplish some truly amazing things. Well, what happens when your head gets big and you start thinking that you're better than others? Something is guaranteed to happen to give you a reality check.

One of my favorite examples of this happened to one of my guests on The Woman Behind the Business Talk Show. My guest was Mrs. Jackie Robinson-Burnette, who was the Senior Executive Service (SES) at the U.S. Small Business Administration serving as the Deputy Associate Administrator, Office of Government Contracting and Business Development. In this capacity, Jackie was one of the highest-ranked executive leaders in the federal government for her profession. One day Jackie, an African-American woman, was preparing a briefing for some of the most powerful men in the world at the Pentagon, in Arlington, Virginia. She was walking through the halls with her "Olivia Pope" walk (for those who remember the hit show Scandal on ABC). She was feeling herself, and if I recall correctly, she was actually thinking things like, "Oh, I must be somebody. The top military commanders are calling on me for a briefing." She continued to strut her stuff as she headed to her briefing—however, Ms. Jackie wasn't accustomed to walking fast in high heels, especially not on the slippery floors of the Pentagon. And when she tells this story she explains that just as quickly as her head started to swell, God dropped her to the floor to remind her that He's in control.

Jackie continued sharing how she collapsed to the floor with her Spanx exposed and her wig crooked, and her mouth wide open in shock at what had happened. But that moment transformed her forever. She no longer walked as though she was better than anyone else. She quickly remembered that it was because of God's grace and other people that she even had the opportunity to serve business owners. From that day forward, she focused her attention on being accessible and approachable. While the fall in this story is quite funny, the parable is powerful. Your character is a huge indicator of how successful you can be. Remember, people like doing business with people they like and, most importantly, trust. When you make it to the top, if you burned bridges and treated people poorly along the way, you'll eventually be sitting pretty and lonely.

A word that I find to be overused more recently is authentic. Everyone seems to tell you to be authentic. What happens when you have been trying to be someone else for so long that you don't know exactly what you authentically look like? I challenge you to ask three people who know you extremely well to share three character traits that define you. I want you to also write down three character traits you believe define you and see if who you believe you are aligns with how others perceive you? This exercise will help you identify your personal brand. It's important to understand how other people see you, as it will allow you to make modifications to areas that you deem necessary. This is a great exercise to do with your company as well. You can ask others what your brand stands for in their eyes. It's a quick and easy way to access improvements around your brand. In today's society of immediate gratification, you will want to be able to address issues around your brand quickly and efficiently. If someone doesn't like an experience your brand is responsible for, they will quickly turn to social media to put your brand on blast.

The only time I turned to social media to oppose a company was when it had to do with a bad travel experience. Have you ever noticed how quickly an airline will respond to criticism or a negative customer relations experience on social media? It's amazing. It's much faster than filing a complaint through their website or trying to call customer service. I can recall traveling an airline and they ended up delaying my flight for four hours because their pilot didn't show up to work. It was horrible for many reasons, mainly because it was supposed to be a 5 a.m. flight and I had been at the airport since 4 a.m. After being declined to go on another flight, I posted about my experience and was quickly accommodated for my troubles.

How would you handle a disappointed customer who takes to social media to put your company on blast? You shouldn't allow negative comments to linger (unaddressed), because then most people will begin to believe the information is true. It is your responsibility, as a business owner, to address the tough situations head on.

The Oversell

Don't oversell your clients. When you are reaching out to individuals, it should be a give and take relationship. No one wants to feel like every time you reach out to them, it's only to sell something.

Not long ago, I was contacted by a young lady on Facebook about being a guest on her podcast about my first book Brand Reppin' 101. I could tell by the language that was written that there would be some type of costs involved with being on her show. But, to be nice, I still replied to her. Shortly after, I received a long, direct message detailing her pricing and the value I would receive from being a part of her platform. I promptly expressed that I wasn't interested, but thanked her for the invitation.

I then inquired about where she lived. She said Florida. I was going to Florida in the next month. I told her it would be nice to possibly connect with her when I'm in town. Her response was something like, "I'll check my availability, but I also want to share a new product I have coming out next year, it'll be available for presale soon." She went on to ask me for my email address. I was so turned off by her response that I just turned my messenger off. Then, I found myself yelling at her (only in my head). I decided to use the opportunity as a teachable moment. Now, everyone might not agree with what I did, but I promise my words came from a place of sincere love, and I honestly want this young lady to win as a business owner. I wrote her back explaining that she was overselling me. I explained that if she wanted to sell me a product that isn't even out yet, she should have accepted my offer to connect when I'm in her town and that she could have presented her pitch to me there. I did my best to convey that I was only sharing because I want her to be successful, and some might say I was out of line, but if you can't accept criticism from a place of true servitude, then you might not be ready to serve others as a business owner.

At the end of the day, you should be sharing information with people to make them want to buy from you. If you're always posting, "Buy my course," or "Purchase my new book," or "Buy my latest product," people will become overwhelmed. They will scroll past your posts or emails because they know you're a one-way communicator. I often tell clients, "Don't be afraid to give away free information." You can tell people how to do anything—most of them will never try to do it, and those that do can never do it like you. So, don't be afraid to package up information and provide it to your clients for free. For instance, last year I started offering monthly marketing minutes. It was a quick, sixty-second snippet about something related to marketing. It allowed me to share the wealth of knowledge that I have around a particular subject while also showing people, "Hey, this is my specialty." You don't have to blatantly ask people to purchase from you. If you show them, it's a lot more powerful.

Let's say you have a product. You can make videos that feature you sharing tips about an industry related to your product. Let's say you have a clothing line. Instead of just featuring your clothing, you might decide to make videos around ways to get stains out of clothing. You could feature your shirt in the video while providing people relevant information about their lives. I'm sure at some point, you have stained your favorite outfit. Why not become a valuable and trusted resource if what you're sharing and showing works?

If this is an area you're not comfortable working in, then you should never be too proud to reach out for help. Having a coach or a mentor to assist you in taking the next steps in business is essential for growth. Asking for help is also a healthy way to let people know you can only go so far in business on your own. You need to assemble a strong team that understands the culture of your business and its mission. Most start-ups and even some businesses have grown past relying solely on themselves to handle all aspects of the business. At some point, if you truly want to grow your business, you'll need to start building a solid team. It's not sustainable for you to manage product development, client interactions, business development, marketing, and billing. If you're attempting to handle it all for a short period of time, that's understandable, but entrepreneurial burnout is real. It was part of the genesis of my creating the Woman Behind the Business Retreat, because I recognized how difficult managing all of the roles of life and business can weigh on a person. You need to take the time to replenish yourself. Your business can't run by itself and neither should you.

Transparency is the one differentiator that can truly set you and your business apart from others. You have the power to make your customers feel valued and safe. By being upfront and honest, you don't leave them guessing or feeling alone on their journey. If you're able to nail transparency, then you're well on your way to building a brand that will last.

Many people are used to not wanting to address problems head-on. They figure if the problems just linger around, they won't do any harm, so they just ignore them. In business, I don't recommend that. You want your brand to scream trustworthy, and in order for it to reach that point, you have to work at it. Congratulations on completing the five phases of your transformation into full-time business ownership.

CHAPTER 9:

Get out of Your Own Way

"Do or do not. There is no try."

– YODA

Congratulations. You have now successfully made it through all of the B.E.A.S.T. Mentality methods. You now have the necessary steps to transition your side hustle into a full-time business. If you took notes as you went through each of the steps, then you have properly aligned yourself and your business for the transition.

But now that you're here, I want to know how you're feeling. You just finished the transparency chapter, so it's important that you truly hone into your feelings. I want you to take a moment to evaluate where you are mentally. Are you amped up and eager to ensure that all of the key components are in place, or have you reverted to thinking about all of the uncertainties that go along with being a business owner? Some of you might have already started freaking out about the financial insecurities that go along with being a business owner. If so, take a moment to think back to my situation of being a divorcee, with two little ones in private school, or how I was forced to sink or swim because my full-time job no longer existed. You see, I used to be in your position. So, what would you do if the company you work for pulls rank and leaves you without a job? How would you cope with that? What is your backup strategy? Would you feel like you would give your business a fair shot? Or would you just seek another job?

The resources that have been created for you in this book were designed to ensure you can be successful throughout every phase of your business career. If right now isn't the best time for you to transition in your life, I totally understand. However, when the time is right, you'll be able to get started building out your business effectively.

Have you ever met a dreamer? You know, someone who often professes their dreams of how they'll be successful, yet they never take the first step toward fulfilling any of their goals? After a while, no matter how serious they might be about starting, people no longer believe they'll ever get started. If you suffer from the anxiety of worrying about what people think, stop. Do not allow the thoughts of others to control your destiny. Don't allow negative outside influences to stifle your growth. If you weren't ready before, but you're anxious and excited to get started today, keep the momentum going—just remember that your why will keep you motivated and encouraged when all hope feels lost. Your why will lift you when you've been told "no" a thousand times.

Did you know that Harland Sanders, better known as Colonel Sanders of Kentucky Fried Chicken, faced rejection 1,009 times before a restaurant accepted his secret chicken recipe? Imagine if Thomas Edison would have given up after his 900th failed attempt at inventing the light bulb. Did you know that Edison made over 1,000 failed attempts before he got it right? The story goes a little something like this: his assistant asked him why he never gave up. Edison apparently replied that he had not failed once. However, he had discovered over 1,000 things that didn't work. These are just some of the many examples of individuals who persevered through the rejection. Imagine how strong Edison's why must have been to remain so diligent through so many failed attempts. Clearly, his mindset helped him through the difficult days. Remember, knowing exactly who you are in this equation is the winning element toward your success.

You see, everyone's road to success isn't easy or pretty. Are you familiar with author J.K. Rowling's story? If you're not familiar with her name, you've heard of her most famous work Harry Potter. Before publishing the series, she was near penniless, divorced, a single mother, and severely depressed. However, in a matter of five years, she went from being welfare-dependent to being one of the richest women in the world.

No matter where you are financially in your life, transitioning into a successful business is possible. One of my favorite segments on The Woman Behind the Business Talk Show is called "The Moments from the Valley." We close out every show with every guest sharing a time in their lives when they didn't know how they'd overcome a particular obstacle. I ask them what the obstacle was, how they transitioned through, and what was waiting for them on the other side.

Over the years, the stories I've heard and have been able to share with the rest of the world have been transformational. One of my favorites was a testimony from a Senior Vice President at an engineering, emergency management, and project management firm. She and her husband endured some pretty humbling times throughout the years of building up their company. One month, they might win a multi-million-dollar federal contract, and the next six months, they might not have any new contracts.

Their business hit a severe drought at one point, which caused them to deplete their savings. Throughout the drought, her husband had been diligently working on an IDIQ proposal that, if they won it, would transition their situation drastically. She recalled all four of their children sleeping in the room with her and her husband for warmth because the gas had been turned off. Her son had even written in his college entrance essay about wanting to get to school early so that he could have heat. Yet, through it all, her husband remained faithful and prayerful through the task.

Once the contract was submitted, they eventually learned they had won the IDIQ which totaled $1.5B. You see, they remained true to their purpose.

"The Moments from the Valley" is my favorite segment because it allows people to see how others have overcome being in some pretty vulnerable situations; yet, it also shows how they made it through. A lot of times people only see what life looks like after individuals have been through a storm, and most people look at the lives they're living and say, "I want to do whatever it is they do." However, you rarely understand their journey to success. Being a business owner is no easy feat, and I'd be doing you a disservice if I didn't make that clear.

However, you have to believe that your success is possible, even if it means going after it alone. The journey can, indeed, feel lonely. But I can assure you that the reward is so worth your hard work and your dedication to the vision.

If making the transformation feels unbearable, you don't have to go at it alone. Our B.E.A.S.T. Mentality program provides you with a dedicated team to assist you throughout the process of transitioning your business. Now that you have been introduced to the system, you have a toolkit of strategies to help structure your side business to a level where you won't use your corporate career as a financial crutch.

If you look over the trajectory of your career and you decide that you're most concerned with managing expectations of family and friends throughout the transition, well, that's a totally valid feeling. But, it shouldn't hinder your growth or pause your transition. If you feel like managing the expectations of others is crippling your progression, it might be time to examine your business model to identify where the apprehension is rooted.

I've worked with a number of clients at varying levels in their career, and the number one element that builds confidence and assertiveness in their business is knowing exactly who they are. The moment your circumstances cause you to forget that one key ingredient, you've already relinquished half of your armor to fear.

Watching my client, Bianca Wise, leave her career as a lieutenant for the Baltimore Fire Department to pursue her dream of owning a company that would nourish her mental, physical, and emotional desire for freedom—well that was powerful. Watching her confidence level shoot up to a place that I had never seen before wasn't only transformational for her, but also for me. I once heard a friend talk about how starting is similar to the birthing process. For any of my women who have children, natural childbirth can bring about excruciating pain, but when the baby arrives, you forget all about the pain. Well, when you are building a business that you believe will positively impact the world, you're going to go through some growing pains. It's not going to be easy, but I promise you, you can do this.

If you don't have a side business, that's okay. If you evaluate where your passion lies, then your purpose shouldn't be too far behind. In Chapter 1, I talked about how we helped align her passion for crafts with teaching others how to utilize crafts to generate revenue. Once she completed the program, she was equipped with the necessary skills to launch and facilitate her crafting courses.

Your business idea doesn't have to have anything to do with the type of work you're currently doing. Your business needs to drive you to want to do more, give more, and be more. When it comes to moving the needle, your business should have some finances to help you get started. However, if you don't have a designated amount of money set aside specifically for your business, that's okay too. You should have zero excuses at this point. However, I know how clever the mind can be, so, if you start thinking that you don't have any formal education in running a business, it's time to rebuke those thoughts.

Think about it from this perspective: when you first started your current job, or any job for that matter, you had to learn their systems and their style for doing things. There's nothing wrong with having a learning curve when you start your business. The main difference between your business and working for an employer is you're structuring your business's standard operating procedures and identifying policies for your team to abide by, establishing what you want the culture of your business to be and crafting the image of your overall brand. Some people are comfortable going along with structures that have already been created. For the most part, that's all most people know until they venture off to establish their own. Think about it. From the time you were in school, you were conditioned to behave a certain way, provide information via a certain process, and you've rarely had an opportunity to explore life beyond the perimeters that were enforced at school or by previous bosses. So quite naturally, it would feel "weird" while you're branching out. You'll most likely question if you're doing things "right," but I encourage you to remember that this baby that you have birthed is yours. Just like parenting—you never know if you're doing things right (and honestly everyone will have an opinion if you allow them to). However, you have to do what feels right for you. That's the beauty of where you are. Embrace it and enjoy the journey—everything you need to be successful already resides within you. The resources and support you need are at your fingertips.

CHAPTER 10:

B.E.A.S.T. Mentality Unleashed

"Never underestimate the power of dreams and the influence of the human spirit. We are all the same in this notion. The potential for greatness lives within each of us."
– WILMA RUDOLPH

nstant gratification seems to be the hot new way of society. Everyone wants everything quickly—insight, answers, and even success. But sometimes people need to take a seat and open their mind and heart, so they can prepare themselves for what the universe has to share with them.

As I retrace my journey, I know that time and silence is exactly what I needed in order to find the inner strength that I had somehow misplaced. Taking a pause was healthy for me. It allowed me to become one with why I decided to write this book, and it granted me permission to reclaim all of the power within me. Not for any benefit of my own, but to ultimately share it with the world and be a blessing to others.

Once I allowed God to order my steps, my pathway landed me right here. I wrote these words when God showed me his will for me. "This book will be a beacon of hope for those who are tired of being captive to their insecurities. I want to be a sounding board for the lady who has put her entire life on pause because she's afraid to walk away from her unhappiness to feel true fulfillment in her purpose. This book was written to provide a foundation for those who haven't heard their story, found their voice, or come across a voice that resonates with them. This book was written to show people that walking a purposeful and truthful life as an entrepreneur is possible."

I've heard amazing business ideas be released from the mouths of thousands, yet only a handful take action. I recognize that even the handful is scared as they decide to no longer be a hostage to their fears. However, they still muster up the courage to keep placing one foot in front of the other.

While my story is slightly different, I still understand what it feels like to be naked to have nothing else as a safety net. I understand what it's like to feel completely vulnerable to your fears and almost controlled by your what-ifs.

When I realized that my truth was more powerful than any of the naysayers or negative thoughts, I was able to build a foundation. I was able to create a story. My story is one of hundreds I have heard over the years. My story is no better or different than the men and women who feel trapped by their circumstances. They are in financial bondage, and their jobs are the way to maintain their happiness, or so they think. I wrote this book because I want people to see that a young black girl from the outskirts of Detroit, Michigan wasn't afraid to bet one hundred percent on herself.

Why should she be?

If you ask someone if they believe in themselves, they'll almost always say, "Of course, I do." But when you ask them to relinquish their safety nets, the truth begins to stabilize. You will hear things like "Well, I don't know if I can," and excuses will shortly follow. But, at the end of the day, no matter what your circumstance is, if you believe in who you are and what you're capable of, there isn't anything that can hold you back from your success.

Your planning phase is essential to the foundation of your business. When you can plan like a boss, then you are ensuring that the structure of your business is solid. You are completing your checklist of requirements to adhere to the parameters of the government in the jurisdiction that the business will be established. This phase protects you from having the business tied directly to your social security number, when you register the business with the IRS and generate your company's EIN. You don't want to miss out on any essential requirements that come with this phase. Take your time as you establish all of the necessary components to building out your business structure.

When it comes to the account method in the B.E.A.S.T. Mentality blueprint, this is the money-maker phase—an essential element to acquiring new clients and generating revenue. You will want to make sure you know your worth when you go about pricing for your products and services. But, in knowing your worth, you also have to know the value of the products and services being offered. I was recently with a dear friend who had purchased some jewelry to support one of our mutual friends. She had purchased the necklace the day before seeing me, but confessed that the necklace broke before she had a chance to wear it. Now, if the necklace was priced around the $10 price point, my friend probably would have just shrugged her shoulders and said, "Welp, you get what you pay for." But she paid $40 for the piece. Imagine her dismay when she had to call our friend to tell her the piece did not hold up to her standards. Knowing your worth is not just about you personally. It's also imperative to know how to price what it is that you're selling. Customers aren't stupid. The goal isn't to get that one sell. Your goal should always be to make the experience worthwhile so you gain a committed customer who will want to support you for life.

Let's keep the example of the necklace in mind. When you've successfully identified your target market, your price point should be in alignment with that market. As an illustration, let's say you consider your brand to be economical fine jewelry, and you're marketing to individuals who currently purchase high-end jewelry. In this example, your slogan is something like, "High quality isn't synonymous with high prices." Well, a prospects decides to give your product a chance, but it breaks before they have a chance to wear it. Now you've just lost a potentially reoccurring client.

Take the time to market as accurately and efficiently as possible. And if you didn't learn anything else from this example, your business all has to flow from one segment to the next. When you have silos in your business, they will slowly suck the productivity out of your business.

Now, let's say when my friend calls our mutual friend to tell her about the necklace, the seller makes excuses. What if she even goes as far as to accuse her of being too rough with the piece? Do you think it's going to make my friend feel good about her purchase? No, she's probably going to feel taken advantage of. However, if she were to call and the seller apologized profusely and offered to replace the piece, my friend probably would have walked away feeling good that she was able to offer feedback to the seller while also getting a new piece. These examples are all about transparency.

Be able to admit your faults and provide immediate solutions that protect your brand's reputation, while also leaving the customer feeling appreciated. Throughout this book, you have seen how every new phase is a continuation of the previous one, just with a focus on a particular aspect of the business. You don't have to have an MBA to understand good customer service and how to attract your customers. You have been a buyer your entire life. Consider some of the things that help you convert from thinking about purchasing something to being transactional. The process is nothing new.

You even have the ability to survey how others like to buy absolutely free using social media. You can run your focus groups by asking your friends and family everything from which logo you like to which slogan resonates most with them. Be strategic with your business dealings so you're not drained from attempting to fulfill all of the roles required to build a money-generating business. You can maintain your hustler status. I just want you to hustle with strategy.

At the top of 2020, I'll celebrate DC Media Connection's fifth anniversary. Has the journey been easy? No. But it's allowed me to see and do some pretty remarkable things. When I decided to soar into entrepreneurship, I went in with a net stretched wide, and I had great intentions. One of the greatest lessons I've learned is that not everyone is your client, nor should they be. When I talk about knowing your target audience, I'm not preaching from a book. I'm sharing from experience. Most new business people are so eager to get a client that they fear turning anyone away. I'm begging you not to do this. If you do, you'll interfere with your ability to effectively reach your ideal client. Think of it this way—every client you take on just for the sake of not wanting to say "no" is stealing space from your ideal client. You know, the one you've clearly defined as part of your target market. I get it. If you don't take on new clients, you could be in jeopardy of going out of business. However, if you're not taking on the right clients, you might still end up losing it all, because you're just attempting to serve everyone as opposed to focusing on what you do best for the clients you know need what you provide.

According to the Bureau of Labor and Statistics, eighty percent of businesses survive their first year, however almost half no longer exist after five years, and only one-third make it past their tenth year.

I've met so many people who have shared flawed reasons for wanting to open a business. They often lead with the appeal of being their own boss, or the allure of the freedom they'll have to do what they want, when they want. But, the truth of the matter is people rarely share the realities of what it takes to be successful in business on social media. This is why I believe a number of people start businesses but, tend to let them go after just a few short years. Mainly because their concept of (what it will take to generate) success was based off someone's insta-stories or series of tweets.

Entrepreneurship is all about being held accountable. As a business owner, you rarely have anyone to hold you accountable, besides your clients. That's why I recommend having an executive committee or even a mentor to assist you through your business management strategies. You need to be surrounded by people who understand where you aspire to be.

Again, I want to see you win. I want you to feel fulfilled every morning when you wake up. If you have been feeling as if you're being held back from something or someone, this is your exodus. It's time to manifest the desires of your heart. I want you to walk in your purpose. If your side hustle brings you happiness, and you feel fulfilled by the products and services you provide…I want to help you experience that sense of joy everyday…especially when you are helping others.

I know there is fear and I know there is uncertainty—I've been there, so, I totally get it. But, I want to share this with you. When I first started my business, I was married. Four years into the business, we're divorced. My story may have started with having someone that I could fall back on, but for the past year I have been one hundred percent reliant on the system I created to ensure that my business could weather the storm. The place that you are in right now, whether you're married, single, have dependents, or are caregiving, I understand. Remember, I'm a full-time business owner with two children. You can do this. Because I'm living proof. You can master this system and build a business that will positively impact society, while also fulfilling you personally and professionally. I know you can do it. You just have to believe in yourself and be willing to bet one hundred percent on you. You've got this.

ACKNOWLEDGMENTS

First, I must acknowledge God, for I know that through him comes my strength, and I am only as good as he allows me to be. I also have to recognize my King and Knight for always being willing to share their mommy with the world.

To all of the women referenced throughout Side Hustle to Main Hustle, thank you for being brave throughout your walk and allowing me to share your story to hopefully be an inspiration and blessing to others.

To my parents, thank you for giving me a name that translates into my life's purpose and for providing me the love and support I needed to truly blossom and own the course that was laid before me.

To my siblings, thank you for always accepting me and all my quirky ways. I appreciate you and the lessons you both have taught me.

To my halfsie, I owe so much of this book to you. Thank you for loving me unapologetically and being my inspiration and motivation during our early morning calls and praying for me when I'm present and when I'm not.

To my favorite flower that would show up at the most unexpected places to remind me that God gave me a special light to draw people closer to him through me. Thank you for the silent whispers when I needed someone to speak to. But, most of all, thank you for keeping me encouraged, grounded, and focused.

A special shout out to the team at DC Radio for all you do to help me craft such a dynamic program for women in business.

I'd also like to give a special thank you to Dr, Angela Lauria and The Author Incubator's team, as well as to David Hancock and the Morgan James Publishing team for helping me bring this book to life.

And last but not least, thank you to all of the amazing women who have mentored me over the years: Mrs. Blackwell, Mrs. Valada Richardson-Sargent, Gail Earle, Stephanie Gaines-Bryant, Kimberly Hardy-Barnes, Angela C. Dingle, Karen M. Alston, and to everyone who has played a role in helping me get to this point in my life, including my ex-husband. Thank you.

THANK YOU

f you've made it to this point in the book, it means one of two things. Either congratulations are in order because you've completed the B.E.A.S.T. Mentality program, or you flipped straight to the back of the book to figure out how many pages are in here. (It's okay, I do it too.)

Regardless of what brought you here, I want you to know how much I appreciate your support. There are probably thousands of books on transitioning into full-time entrepreneurship, so I'm grateful you selected *Side Hustle to Main Hustle: The Owner's Manual to Full-Time Entrepreneurship* to aid you on your journey.

As a thank you, I'd like to invite you to experience a free Side Hustle to Main Hustle online class. To access the course, just email freeclass@angelnlivas.com. If you feel like you're not ready to rock and roll just yet or if you have a few strategy questions you'd like a little counsel on, not a problem. You can schedule a complimentary session with me online at www.dcmc.as.me/Discovery.

Let's stay connected on your favorite social media platforms: @angelnlivas.

ABOUT THE AUTHOR

Angel N. Livas is a best-selling author, visionary, CEO, and 2019 Communicator award recipient for her radio program, "The Woman Behind The Business Talk Show."

In 2016, Angel organized a movement for women entrepreneurs to expand their companies into international territories by way of her non-profit, "The Woman Behind The Business." Since its inception, women from across the globe annually convene in Nassau, Bahamas, where the first international chapter was formed.

As the CEO of DC Media Connection, Angel utilizes her keen sense of video production and content creation to attract her clients to their ideal consumers. Recently, Angel was named "Woman to Watch 2020 for Business Excellence" by the Creative Life Institute. In 2016, Angel was highlighted in the Washington Business Journal under

"People On The Move" and named "Influential Business Woman of 2016" by AI Magazine.

Before embarking upon her entrepreneurial journey, Angel oversaw six-nationally syndicated talk-radio shows, which included producing programming for award-winning celebrity hosts Larry King and Jane Pauley.

Today, she uses storytelling as a tool to connect to the hearts of audiences as she graces global stages from Accra, Ghana, to moderating conversations throughout the Caribbean. Angel is a proud lady of Alpha Kappa Alpha Sorority, Incorporated, and a graduate of Howard University, where she graduated magna cum laude. She received her Master of Arts from the American University and she is also the recipient of two professional certifications from Stanford University and Rutgers University. Angel currently resides in Northern Virginia with her two children.

CPSIA information can be obtained
at www.ICGtesting.com
Printed in the USA
JSHW061812191222
35156JS00001B/66

9 781631 951077